Scenic Byways
of
Northern California

From the Siskiyous to the Cascades

Marie Webster Weisbrod
Illustrated by Connie Van Pelt

Naturegraph Publishers

Library of Congress Cataloging-in-Publication Data

ISBN 0-87961-265-7

Copyright © 2002 by Marie Webster Weisbrod
Copyright © 2002 illustrations by Connie Van Pelt

All rights reserved. Printed in the United States by Mosaic Press. No part of this book may be used or reproduced without prior written permission of the publisher.

Naturegraph Publishers has been publishing books on natural history, Native Americans, and outdoor subjects since 1946. Please write for our free catalog.

Books for a better world

Naturegraph Publishers, Inc.
PO Box 1047 • 3543 Indian Creek Rd
Happy Camp, CA 96039
(530) 493-5353
www.naturegraph.com

ACKNOWLEDGMENTS

When a writer travels, strangers become friends, and friends become valuable sources of inspiration and information. Without their assistance, a guide book such as this one could not have been produced. I am most appreciative of those who encouraged me to pursue the project from its inception: Karen and Mark O'Rourke, Klamath Riverside RV Park, Orleans; Clara and Don Stewart, Sidney Gulch RV Park, Weaverville; Jean and Eddie Davenport, Elk Creek Campground, Happy Camp; Sheri and Dave Overly of Carrville Inn, Trinity Center; Bill and Tom Miranda, Old Lewiston Bridge RV Resort, Lewiston.

Many others I met along the way offered suggestions, and patiently answered numerous questions via snail mail, e-mail, or phone when I returned home. My gratitude goes to the personnel and volunteers in Chambers of Commerce, visitor centers, museums and newspaper offices: Nita Rowley and Glen North, Willow Creek; Shirley Reynolds, Orleans; Judy Bushy and Linda Martin, Happy Camp; Beth Franklin, Scott Valley Alpacas, Greenview.

Skip Taylor, Butte Valley, Dorris; Karen Heiser, Weed; Joanne Steele and Judy Taylor, Siskiyou County; Karen Whitaker, Shasta Cascade; Scott Lawson and Evelyn Whisman, Plumas County. National forest service rangers and public affairs officers in every county were most helpful in supplying information; especially Mary Lou Schmierier, Interpretive Specialist, Lassen County. A special thank-you to Jeanne Burrer of the Karuk Tribe in Happy Camp for sending newsletters, and Jill M. Sherman, Native American Heritage Commission, for the copy of *In Hoopa Territory* . It has been a pleasure to work with Barbara Brown, publisher of Naturegraph, and Connie Van Pelt, artist and illustrator. My thanks to Julie Leigh of Chico State University for editing the manuscript. None of this could have been accomplished without the love and support of my sons, Kurt and Eric Weisbrod, and their lovely wives, Kris and Connie.

I have been asked if I am a descendant of Daniel Webster. Although he was a respected senator from Massachusetts during the 1830s and 40s, after reading what he said about the West, I would not claim him as an ancestor.

"What do we want of this worthless area, this region of savages and wild beasts? To what use could we ever hope to put these great deserts and these endless mountain ranges?"

My Webster ancestors were Scots-Irish flax growers and weavers from County Armagh, Ireland. Although they settled in the Catskills (where I was born) they would have felt at home in the Siskiyou and Klamath Mountains, the Trinity Alps and the Cascade Range. As do I.

Marie Webster Weisbrod

TABLE OF CONTENTS

Acknowledgements 3

Introduction 9

Part One: Northwestern California

1. The People and the Land 15
2. Smith River Scenic Byway 23
3. Trinity River Scenic Byway 33
4. Big Foot Scenic Byway 49
5. State of Jefferson Scenic Byway 65
6. Trinity Heritage Scenic Byway 83

Part Two: Northeastern California

7. The People and the Land 103
8. Modoc Volcanic Scenic Byway 111
9. Shasta Volcanic Scenic Byway 123
10. Lassen Volcanic Scenic Byway 135

Bibliography 145

Sources of Information for each of the Byways 149

LIST OF ILLUSTRATIONS

Part One: Northwestern California

Chapter II. Smith River Scenic Byway map 22
   1. Tolowa House 24
   2. California Coast Redwood 26
   3. Darlingtonia californica 29
   4. Patrick Creek Lodge 31

Chapter III. Trinity River Scenic Byway map 32
   5. Shasta State Historic Park Museum 34
   6. Weaverville's Spiral Staircase 41
   7. Tree Swallow and California Dipper 45

Chapter IV. Bigfoot Scenic Byway map 48
   8. Jedediah Smith Monument 53
   9. Bigfoot, human and bear paw prints 57
  10. Lady slipper and nuthatch 62

Chapter V. State of Jefferson Scenic Byway map 64
  11. The American House/Cuddihy Hotel 69
  12. Douglas Fir and Brewer's Spruce cones . . . 72
  13. The Wildwood 75
  14. Great Blue Heron 76
  15. Horse Creek Suspension Bridge 78
  16. Ash Creek Bridge, 1901 80

Chapter VI. Trinity Heritage Scenic Byway map 82
    17.   Fort Jones Museum 86
    18.   Callahan Ranch Hotel 90
    19.   Bowerman Barn, 1878 96
    20.   Old Lewiston church and cemetery 99

Part Two: Northeastern California

Chapter VIII. Modoc Scenic Byway map 110
    21.   Byway signs 115
    22.   Lava beds and Juniper tree 118
    23.   Bald Eagle 120

Chapter IX. Shasta Volcanic Scenic Byway map 122
    24.   Visitor center sign 124
    25.   Mt. Shasta and Living Memorial
            Sculpture Garden 128

Chapter X. Lassen Volcanic Scenic Byway map 134
    26.   Seismograph 137
    27.   Roop's Fort 143

Town Maps

Weaverville, Trinity River Scenic Byway 34

Willow Creek, Bigfoot Scenic Byway 50

Happy Camp, State of Jefferson Scenic Byway 67

INTRODUCTION

*Two roads diverged in a wood, and I -
I took the one less traveled by,
And that has made all the difference.*
                                        Robert Frost

How many back-road travel writers have quoted the rural philosopher, his words resonating in our hearts and minds? A half century ago he spoke for all of us—the wanderer, the nomad, the gypsy—although this may not have been his intent.

Robert Frost's roads wound through woods of birch, bordered by stone walls enclosing farms and barns and cow pastures. My roads wind around mountains so high, they would dwarf the hills of New England. Yet the image behind the poet's words is the same—lovely stretches of road leading into unknown territory.

One of these remote regions can be found in Northern California, west of I-5 and east of Highway 101; a tangled mass of ranges, bound to earth by mountain meadows and alpine lakes, where rivers have slashed a labyrinth of gorges through granite boulders. Five scenic byways, circling around the Siskiyou and Klamath mountains and the Trinity Alps, encompass this awesome landscape.

Another region lies below the Oregon border east of I-5 to the Nevada state line and stretches south along the Cascade Range to encircle Mt. Shasta and Lassen Peak. Three scenic byways twist around these volcanic mountains, and the caves, cinder cones, and lava-strewn landscape that resulted from their eruptions.

Although I'm not a native-born westerner, I am a mountain person. For many years I hiked and backpacked through the wilderness surrounding the village where I live in the San Jacinto Mountains of Southern California. Here the whims of nature move gently, brushing the peaks with winter white snows, painting foothills with wild blue lilac to herald spring, carpeting the pine and cedar forest with purple lupine in summer, and touching oak leaves golden yellow when the nights are crisp.

In such a perfect place, why leave home? Just like "the bear who went over the mountain, to see what he could see," I, too, am blessed (or cursed?) with an insatiable wanderlust. Although I had explored, in my camper-van, nearly every back road of the southern portion of our state, from the Laguna and San Bernardino mountains to the Coast Range and the Sierra Nevada, I had never ventured into that unknown topography printed in huge blocks of green on the map of Northern California. Frankly, my first approach was white-knuckled.

I found no tourist traps along the byways; no shopping malls, high-rise condominiums or fancy black-tie resorts; no theme parks, giant water slides or I-Max theaters; no huge buses disgorging hordes of people—and no traffic jams. And isn't that the fun of it? Especially for travelers who delight in wandering "off-the-beaten-path," experiencing a different natural environment, learning about the natives who once roamed the countryside and about the explorers who trod their trails.

The book is divided into two sections: Northwestern and Northeastern California. In the opening chapters of each section, I have provided historical information to add dimension to your trip. As you drive these byways and note the names of trailblazers and the emigrants who followed in their wake, these brief additions may be appreciated. You will visit Indian reservations and browse their museums; linger in historic inns and share stories with fellow travelers; have picnics beside the rivers and perhaps cast a line in their waters; swim in placid pools or raft in the riffles; camp under towering pines and hike trails through deep woods.

You'll find remnants of old-growth forest, wildflowers in the meadows, sunbeams casting shadows over blacktop, and showers arching rainbows from peak to peak. You might spot blue herons standing long-legged on riverbanks and hear the plop of steelhead trout in the water, watch a bald eagle soar, and, maybe, catch sight of Bigfoot skulking through the woods. *Bigfoot?* Man or animal? Myth or legend?

Precautions: Before you leave, check road conditions at www.dot.ca.gov/hq/roadinfo or phone (800) 427-7625. The twisting, narrow two-lane roads that comprise these eight scenic byways are tough on itineraries and impossible for a tight time schedule. But what's the hurry? Be flexible. Your drive may be a solitary one or you might have a logging truck or a forest ranger riding your bumper—but no one will honk impatiently. (Do pull over in the turnouts and let them go by! This is their territory and they are not on vacation.)

Deer may leap in front of your car or a fox may scurry across the road. Rocks can tumble down steep hillsides, especially after rains. There undoubtedly will be delays, controlled traffic, and detours on one-way lanes due to landslides and necessary road repairs. Drive these byways slowly and marvel at their construction. Then marvel at the natives and explorers, fur trappers and gold miners, mule team and stagecoach drivers, pioneers and settlers who navigated them before they were cut through rocky defiles, banked, and paved.

After my initial trepidation at venturing along the remote routes of Northern California, envisioning a travel guide to the byways was easy; to visit them again, a joy; to evaluate my favorite places, difficult. It should be surmised that the byways can be driven in directions other than those I have traveled. My choices were based upon the most scenic route or on the direction blazed by the explorers. The adventure lies in the journey, rather than a destination. If you drive these scenic byways, you'll discover your own favorite sites and scenes and, I hope, be enriched by the experience—as I was—and will return again—as I have.

PART ONE:
NORTHWESTERN CALIFORNIA

Chapter I
THE PEOPLE AND THE LAND

In the spring of 1828, Jedediah Strong Smith, with a brigade of 19 trappers, slogged his way up California's central valley, setting beaver traps in the rivers as they traveled. Incredibly, they were herding 300 horses and mules that they hoped to sell at the annual rendezvous of fur hunters at Bear Lake in the Utah Territory. As they sought a way to the Pacific Ocean, they crossed the Sacramento River and turned westward. It would not be an easy jaunt. Before them rose a massive barrier of metamorphosed volcanic and granite formations, uplifted and warped by faults, scoured and gouged by ancient glaciers, bisected and eroded by snowmelt rivers.

On April 13, Jedediah Smith wrote in his journal: *My route was in the direction of a Gap of the Mountain through which I intended to pass . . . The country verry rough and hilly.* This was merely the beginning of a two-month-long ordeal, traversing the Trinity Alps. Four days and some 30 miles later: *Then crossing the ridge of the Mountain where there was some snow and high peaks . . . I came to waters that ran North West.* Following present-day Hayfork Creek, the trappers had stumbled upon the South Fork of the Trinity River.

On April 20 Smith noted: *I had to travel along the side of the hills through thickets of Brush and over steep and rough masses of rock. The travelling extremely bad was made more difficult and dangerous by the great number of horses which I had along. In a bad pass the horses endeavored to avoid being crowded off themselves and therefore rushed against whatever opposed them. Several of my horses pushed from a precipice into the river and drowned.*

Rain and snow plagued the explorers; they found no game to resupply dwindling stores of dried meat, their horses went lame from the rough terrain, and forage for the animals was sparse. They stumbled through thick forests of cedar and pine, forded streams clogged with vine maple and willow trees, fought their way through dense undergrowth of chaparral and blackberry bushes, scrambled over boulders slippery with moss and fungus, confronted bobcats and mountain lions, and were mauled by bears.

These obstacles to progress might be seen as minimal compared to encounters with the natives through whose land they were trespassing. The Wintun Indians, the largest tribe in Northern California, inhabited the territory west of the Sacramento River to the crest of the Coast Range. *They had their bows strung and their arrows in their hands and by the violence of their gestures, their constant yelling and their refusal to come to me left no doubt on my mind of their inclination to be hostile. I therefore in order to prevent them from doing me further injury fired on them.*

This was a hostile welcome for the explorers to this mountainous region until they followed the Trinity River northward. *In the morning several indians came to camp different from the indians I had before seen in the country, particulary in their dress. These indians were clothed in Deer Skin . . . and some of them had Mockasins. Their lodges were . . . 10 to 12 feet square, the sides 3 feet high and the roof shaped like a house . . . and they had a few good canoes.*

And they were friendly. Were they Hupas, Karuks or Yuroks? The Hupas occupied an eight-mile-long fertile valley watered by the Trinity River and enclosed by thickly forested hillsides. Karuk villages were scattered from the confluence of the Trinity with the Klamath River northeast to the Oregon Territory, Smith's ultimate destination. Yurok land stretched northwest along the Klamath, over the Coast Range to the sea, the route that Smith followed. If he had thought the Trinity Alps country was tough going, it was relatively easy compared to the Klamath River Canyon.

A month after leaving the Sacramento Valley, Smith wrote: *Crossing a deep rocky ravine I found greater obstacles than I had before encountered in that rough country . . . and by night had made but two miles. Two of my horses were dashed to pieces from the precipices and many others terribly mangled . . . My men were almost as weak as the horses for the poor venison contained verry little nourishment.*

In hopes of finding a more direct route to the ocean, Smith and his men left the riverbanks to head overland, took one look at the impossible terrain along the coast, and went back to the river. It was the middle of June before the party finally reached the mouth of the Klamath, with no luck obtaining beaver except those acquired by trade with the natives. The expedition trudged on into Oregon, only to be ambushed in July on the Umpqua River. Smith and two of his men were the only survivors of the massacre.

This mountain man, born at the end of the eighteenth century, moved westward to St. Louis at age 23 and found work with the Ashley-Henry Fur Trading Company. His first journeys were by boat up the Missouri River, following the path blazed by Lewis and Clark in 1805. By age 27, Jedediah Smith was leader of his own expedition, the first to travel overland to California, crossing the Great Basin and the Sierra Nevada Mountains, and the first to travel up the coast into Oregon. At age 32 an Indian's arrow ended his travels. About his life, he wrote: *I of course expected to find beaver . . . but I was also led on by the love of novelty common to all which is much increased by the pursuit of its gratification.*

During the two decades after Smith's return to the north country, explorers by the dozens pushed their way over the Siskiyou Mountains, seeking an inland route into California. A member of the 1841 Wilkes Mapping Expedition wrote: *The whole mountainside is admirably adapted for an ambuscade, . . . almost too steep for brush to grow . . . and in many places too narrow for a rabbit to walk over.* Other emigrants struggled south from the Oregon Trail, crossed the barren lands of northeastern California, and followed the Pit River into the central valley.

One of these emigrants was Pierson B. Reading, who established a rancho on the Sacramento River at the mouth of Cottonwood Creek. When gold was discovered in the Sierra Nevada Mountains, he reasoned the streams to the west should also be prospected for the precious metal. After making the first gold strike on a tributary of the Trinity River, he returned for some serious mining with a group of three other white men and sixty Indians, a herd of a 120 cattle, and an ample supply of provisions. After digging countless shovels of dirt, washing it in crude boxes mounted on rockers, Reading's laborers had sifted some 4,000 ounces of gold, worth $20 per ounce in 1848.

When word spread of Reading's success, gold seekers by the hundreds scrambled north from the Sierra Mother

Lode, south from the Oregon Territory, and eastward from San Francisco, all feverishly seeking the big bonanza. Within four years, prospectors had mined every stream flowing through the Trinity and Klamath mountains, leaving piles of tailings along the banks.

As I ponder the result of those four years, it seems obvious the natives would not have taken kindly to this invasion. Disease and murder decimated the tribes, their streams were torn asunder by the gold diggers, and their homeland was nearly destroyed. When the Wintuns retaliated and killed a white man, they were tracked by a sheriff's posse south along Hayfork Creek. One of the group's scouts, standing atop a natural limestone bridge spanning the creek, sighted Indian campfires upstream. At dawn, the posse made their way along the narrow draw and slaughtered 150 natives in the Bridge Gulch Massacre.

Though still sparsely populated, I found this mountainous region much easier to traverse than the first explorers did. Jedediah Smith had crossed the Sacramento River north of Red Bluff, his route into and over the Trinities roughly paralleling Highway 36. Present day travelers track the Old Trinity Trail, the route of pack trains hauling supplies to miners and stagecoaches transporting settlers. Highway 299 now effortlessly mounts passes and drops gently into the valleys below. But the vista off to the west is the same—rough and rugged, sharply peaked—and still wild.

The spark that spurred preservation of these wildlands flared in 1891 with the development of Forest Preserves, their boundaries to be established by Congress. The name was changed in 1907 to National Forests and placed under the jurisdiction of the U. S. Department of Agriculture, to be managed by the forest service. Over two million acres of forest and grasslands were divided into 10 regions, the mission "to achieve quality land management under sustainable multiple-use to meet the diverse needs of the people."

Of the 156 National Forests nationwide, 18 are in California and, of these, three are included in Part One of this guide: nearly a million acres of the Six Rivers National Forest, almost two million acres of the Klamath National Forest, and more than two million acres of the Shasta-Trinity National Forest. Within these forests are four areas designated Wilderness, due to the formation of the Wilderness Society in 1935 and to the National Wilderness Preservation System, created by Congress in 1964. Twenty years later, the California legislature passed its own Wilderness Act.

These natural, primitive areas in Northern California include 153,000 acres of the Siskiyou Wilderness, 440,000 acres in the Marble Mountain Wilderness, 12,000 acres in the Russian Wilderness, and 410,000 acres of the Trinity Alps Wilderness. The objective of their isolation is "to retain the primeval character of the land, with the imprint of humans minimal or unnoticeable."

The law further seeks to protect these undeveloped lands from "high impact" activities, such as timber cutting, road building, the use of motorized vehicles and, in some cases, grazing of livestock. "Low impact" activities—hunting, fishing, hiking, and camping—are declared legitimate uses of the wilderness. Permits may be required to enter some areas and can be obtained at the forest service offices listed in the appendix.

Four "wild and scenic" rivers flow through the wondrous landscape of Northwestern California. As I traced their courses, I discovered the original motivation for river preservation came from opposition to the continued building of dams in 1967–1968. Guidelines were developed by the Department of Agriculture and Department of the Interior in 1970, with potential entries suggested by Congress or by state governors. To be considered eligible, "a river that possesses . . . remarkable scenic, recreational, geologic, fish and wildlife, historic and cultural qualities . . . shall be preserved in free-flowing condition." In 1972, several Northern California rivers were included in a state scenic rivers system, and in 1980 national designation was requested for the Smith, Klamath, Scott, and Salmon rivers, and the Trinity River with its tributaries. As you drive along their banks or kayak in their riffles or photograph a waterfall, you will be grateful for their protected status.

The Smith River and its contributing forks and streams drains the western slopes of the Siskiyou Mountains. The Klamath, running south from Oregon's Crater Lake, spills from Iron Gate Dam to the Pacific Ocean—175 miles of prime fishing and rafting water. The Salmon River, running through a steep-walled canyon from the Trinity Alps Primitive Area, includes 25 miles of the North

Fork, 17 miles of the South Fork, and 21 miles to its confluence with the Klamath. The Scott River, flowing 68 miles from its headwaters in the Marble Mountain Wilderness, has 24 miles designated "wild and scenic" before its junction with the Klamath. The Trinity River's 203 miles from the Lewiston Dam to its confluence with the Klamath, including the North and South forks and the New River, includes 44 "wild" miles, 39 "scenic" miles, and 120 miles for "recreational purposes."

Five scenic byways track and encircle these river systems. The requirements for their designation are extremely detailed; not only must they be scenic but they should also offer natural, historical, cultural, archaeological, or recreational features. The process is lengthy and time-consuming. Five governmental agencies may designate an eligible road: the National Forest Service, the National Park Service, the Bureau of Land Management, the Bureau of Indian Affairs, and the Department of Transportation. Recommendations are reviewed by a panel of experts every two years.

The byways covered in Part One of this guide include 32 miles of the Smith River Scenic Byway, 140 miles of Trinity River Scenic Byway, 108 miles of State of Jefferson Scenic Byway, and 120 miles of Trinity Heritage Scenic Byway. The newest route, 88 miles of Bigfoot Scenic Byway, approved in August 2000, involved eight years of commitment by the sponsors and their supporters.

Bigfoot or Sasquatch, for whom this latest byway is named, was first sighted by a logging crew along the Bluff Creek tributary of the Klamath River in the summer of 1958. Descriptions have evolved from more than 800 sightings throughout the Northwest: a huge, bipedal creature eight to ten-feet tall with a heavy dark-haired torso, its head set directly on its shoulders with a flat nose and sloping forehead, long hands and arms—and big feet. Although allegedly photographed in 1967, no physical evidence has been found: only plaster casts of footprints.

Who or what is this creature? Theories abound. It might be a relic humanoid, a divergent line of the Neanderthal man, or a surviving form of orangutan. Whatever its origin, interest in Bigfoot has continued and, as publicity increased, more sightings have been reported throughout the Northwest. In the fall of 1998, *The Trinity Journal* recorded a sighting in the Hayfork area; the following winter, *Skeptic Magazine* ran an article claiming the 1968 film was a hoax, yet an article in *Field and Stream*, January 2000, presented the possibility that the footprints were genuine.

I can't help but wonder if Jedediah Smith and his men ever spotted Bigfoot lurking in the woods, watching their stumbling progress along boulder-clogged canyons—boulders he or she could surmount in a single leap. As you drive around these byways, wander the trails and rest in the waysides, raft on the rivers or camp in the forest, stay alert; keep your binoculars and camera at hand. Perhaps you will take the photograph of *this* century.

22 « SCENIC BYWAYS

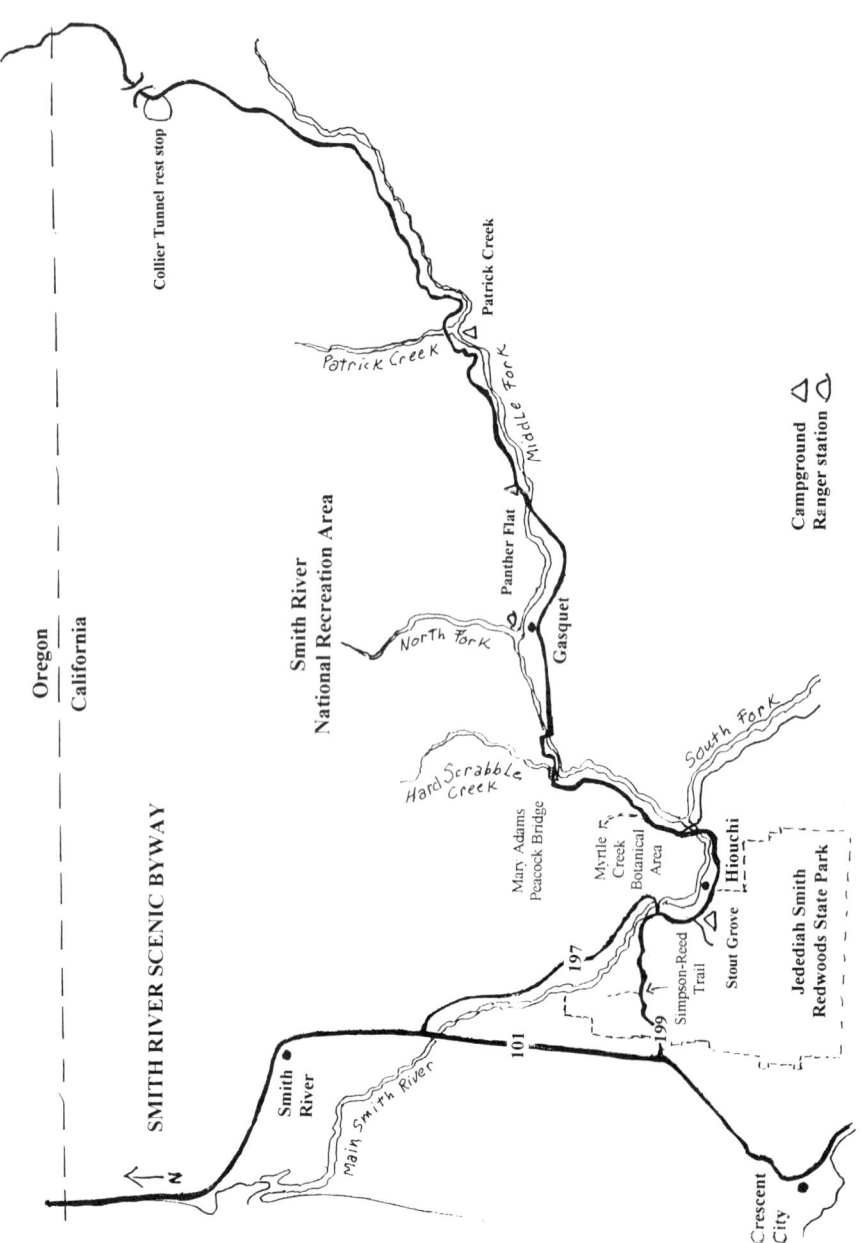

Chapter II
SMITH RIVER SCENIC BYWAY
U.S. Highway 199
32 Miles

On June 20, 1828, three grueling months after leaving the Sacramento Valley, Jedediah Smith came to the river that honors his name today and wrote in his journal: *Crossed a river 80 yards wide coming from the ESE*. Brief mention for what would be California's only free-flowing river, with no dam to stop its 300 miles of streams and tributaries. But to Smith it was probably just "one more river to cross" before finally reaching Oregon Territory.

Biographers have used such terms as "intrepid" or "courageous" when writing of Smith's adventures. To me, he was one gutsy guy. To commemorate his exploits, Smith's name dignifies not only the river but a 305,000-acre national recreation area, a 9,500-acre state park, a 32 mile scenic byway, and the town of Smith River, declaring itself the "Easter Lily Capital of the World."

When Smith and his troops set up camp beside his river, they encountered a tribe of natives who *give us help, bringing us clams and fish, raspberries and the Camas root*. These friendly natives were the Tolowas, a name alien to the people but attached to them by white men. No tribe as such existed but merely a collection of villages that had thrived for centuries inland from the Pacific Ocean; the He-nag-gi lived along the lower Smith River, the Toli-o-wa around a nearby lake, and the Ta-ta-ten on the coast.

Rectangular-shaped houses of wood and stone, built partially into the ground, provided some protection from persistent wind, rain, and fog. An abundance of food supplies surrounded them: wild onions, mushrooms, and the potato-like Camas roots; blackberries, raspberries, and huckleberries; acorns that were stone-ground into a powdery meal supplemented by clams, mussels, salmon, smelt, and eel. Every year the Tolowas hosted fish camps on the beach, roasting or smoking their catch over wood

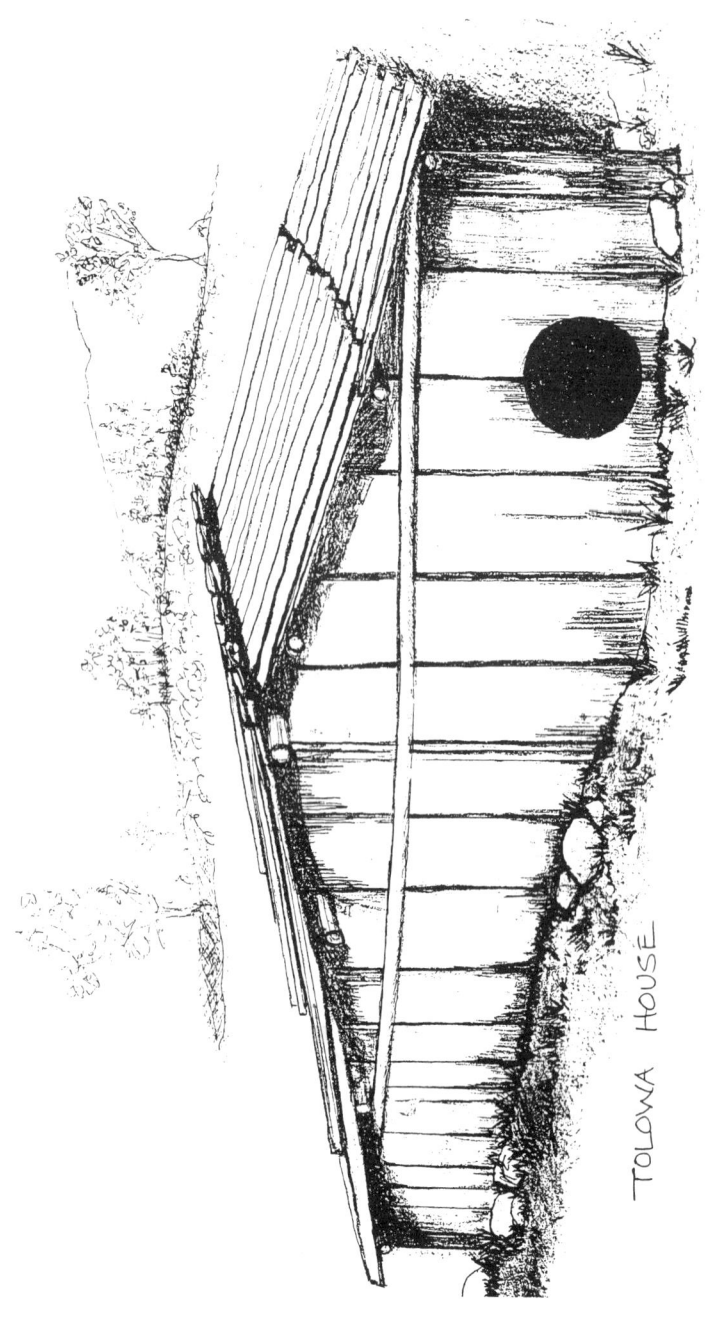

fires or steaming it on hot rocks in reed-woven cooking baskets. Dressed in garments decorated with abalone and dentalia shells, they celebrated the harvest with ceremonial dances. Demonstrations of these rituals can be observed today on special occasions within the Redwood National and State parks along the Northern California coast.

For your exploration of these parks, drive Highway 101 four miles north of Crescent City and turn east on Highway 199. The Smith River Scenic Byway begins at this junction. Although the route traverses four miles of redwoods, the only way to appreciate what John Steinbeck called "ambassadors from another time" is to walk among them. Watch for signs to the Simpson-Reed Trail on the left side of the road, with ample parking for all vehicles, even big RVs.

As you follow the path through the forest, your bootsteps muffled by spongy layers of duff, breathe the musky scent of loamy soil, the spicy aroma of wild ginger, and the fragrant blooms of the Western azalea. Watch for sprays of pink lady's slipper orchids and pale green sprigs of maidenhair fern hiding in the shelter of flowering dogwood.

Whether you are camping or not, your next stop should be Jedediah Smith State Park, entrance on your right. For my first visit, I parked the camper-van in a tree-sheltered niche and walked to the visitor center to gather information about campfire programs and park trails. After tracing a path winding along the riverfront, I crossed a footbridge at the east end of the park that led me to the Stout Grove of redwoods. At the base of a 345-foot masterpiece, I shucked my daypack, leaned against its grooved, red trunk and gazed skyward. Its sheer mass induced a peaceful feeling of immortality—and an unsettling feeling of vertigo.

If you visit Stout Grove and think it all looks vaguely familiar, you wouldn't be wrong. This deep, haunted, shadowy wood was the setting for *Star Wars: Return of the Jedi.*

After leaving the state park and heading east, stop at the Hiouchi Information Center on the left of Highway 199. Here you can acquire a complete collection of materials about the national park: all the rules and regulations; what to wear in the drippy environment and what to do with your pet; where you can fish, camp and hike, ride

your bicycle or horse, and how not to get lost; which plants are protected and where to stash your litter; and how to avoid wild animals, ticks, and poison oak. You will also be warned of possible trail closures and road delays due to rock slides and repairs. You can buy postcards to send home; purchase a ream of trail maps, field guides, and books on the natural and human history of the region; and learn everything you could wish to know about the coast redwoods.

On May 19, 1828, Jedediah Smith recorded seeing these magnificent trees for the first time: *Some of the Cedars were the noblest trees I had ever seen being 12 or 15 feet in diameter, tall, straight and handsome.* A century ago, the trails he followed were encompassed by two million acres of old-growth forest. Two decades after his passing, trees were toppled by the hundreds and the whining saw of loggers shattered the primeval silence. Today, only 4 percent remains. If it hadn't been for the formation of Save-the-Redwoods League in 1918, and the establishment of Redwood National Park in 1968, all would be gone.

The term "old-growth forest" refers to more than redwoods and includes 20-plus species of cone-bearing evergreens over 200 years old. Among them are the Douglas fir, with its dark-gray bark and raggedy cones, and Sitka spruce, with its stems covered in needles growing in spirals. The most revered of these conifers is the redwood. Since they do not have taproots, it is their sheer mass that keeps them upright, providing a canopy for shade-loving trees such as the tanoak, red alder, big leaf maple, and the red-barked madrone. These, in turn, shelter ground-covering mosses and lichens, ferns and berry bushes, and the colorful rhododendron.

A great variety of forest creatures skitter in and among the shrubs: wood rats and deer mice, rabbits and reptiles, bats and insects. Dependent upon nature's bounty is the controversial spotted owl. A mating pair nests in the tops of large hollow trees—and they are choosy. In order to gather enough food for its young, a pair of owls needs a 100 acres of old-growth forest. Declared an endangered species by the U.S. Fish and Wildlife Service, conflict raged between timber companies and conservationists—especially within the territory of the coast redwoods.

When you leave the state park boundaries heading east and cross the first bridge over the river, you will pass Hiouchi (*hi-ooh-chee*; high, clear water). This wee burg offers a post office, a motel, and a cafe serving "blue-ribbon clam chowder."

Just beyond Hiouchi, the South and Middle forks of the Smith River join the main stem, flowing 16 miles north to dump into the ocean. The road along the South Fork is a paved scenic drive leading to river access points and numerous trails for backpackers and serious hikers. One of these is the Kelsey Trail built in the 1850s as a mule-train route between Crescent City and Fort Jones, 200 miles to the east over the mountains.

Eastward bound, watch for signs designating the Myrtle Creek Botanical Area, where many rare plant species thrive. Park in the pullout on the right side of the byway and cross the road to the trailhead for a two-mile round-trip easy walk along Myrtle Creek. In its waters, an old miner discovered a 47 ounce gold nugget over a century ago, resulting in a flurry of hydraulic mining. The trail follows a ditch constructed to draw from the creek the huge amounts of water necessary for the process. Along the way, interpretive signs describe the destruction on the hillsides caused by the operation, and the remarkable recovery of the diverse plant communities.

As you follow the scenic byway beside the Middle Fork, you will soon understand why this tumultuous river is called "a one-way street." With headwaters fed by torrential rains (100 inches a year) high in the Siskiyou Mountains, these waters do not encourage travel upriver from the sea to the interior. Even the broken-back, stream-creased patch of land it flows through does not lend itself to easy driving.

From this point, the highway jogs northeast in sharp curves, the river crunched by the soaring canyon walls of the Middle Fork Gorge. You have now entered the Smith River National Recreation Area, that huge yellow-green arrowhead-shaped mass on the Northern California state map. In a series of congressional acts, the Smith River basin progressed from reserve status in the Klamath National Forest in 1907, to part of the newly created Six Rivers National Forest in 1947, to becoming a National Recreation Area in 1990.

Along the way to the district ranger's headquarters in Gasquet, you will pass several river access points for foolhardy boaters, the junction of Hard Scrabble Creek, and will cross the river on the first bridge in California to be named for a woman. Mary Adams Peacock was so honored for the hospitality she offered wayfarers at her lodging facilities. The road then travels through the few acres of privately owned land in the entire region and, after the North Fork of the Smith River swooshes into the main stem, deposits you in Gasquet (*gas-kay*). Named for the French settler Horace Gasquet, the village was advertised in the late 1800s as "The Finest Summer Resort in Northern California."

A must stop here is the district ranger station built in 1938 by the Civilian Conservation Corps (CCC), beautifully maintained and staffed by forest service employees. Check out the photo of the station as it looked when first built and browse the shelves of nature books, travel guides, and maps of the area. An eight-page pamphlet gives directions to more than 70 miles of trails that wander off into the mountains, detailing mileage, degree of difficulty, descriptions of each trail, and a list of backcountry campsites. A variety of brochures describe fishing holes, swimming beaches, "put-in" points for rafters and kayakers, and the three campgrounds along the river. Panther Flats, two miles east of the Gasquet Station, is the largest of the forest service campgrounds (open year-round) and a good place for a picnic with a splendid view of the river.

Before leaving the station, take a peek at (or a photo of) the large display boards showing the history of the natives and the pioneers who settled this rugged country. The old, unpaved Gasquet Toll road, leading north into Oregon, takes off just beyond the station and is a favorite backcountry trip for four-wheelers.

My next recommended stop is just a couple of miles past the ranger station. Watch for signs and a parking lot for the Darlingtonia Trail, a short, easy stroll through an unusual ecological terrain. Follow a boardwalk over the wet, spongy ground to two platforms providing an overview of the California pitcher plants, which obtain nutrients from the insects and other small organisms trapped within their light-green cobra-shaped leaves.

DARLINGTONIA CALIFORNICA

Another four miles farther east is admittedly my favorite of all the many wonderful attractions on this most scenic of byways. What should I suggest you do first? Since the Patrick Creek picnic area and campground on the right-hand side of the road is easy to access, pull into the parking lot and explore.

In the 1930s, on the banks of the Middle Fork at the junction of Patrick Creek, the CCC created rock walls and walkways, fire pits and comfort buildings, many of which exist today. You can catch a bit of sun on the beach or launch a raft or inner tube in the clear, green waters. A brochure titled "Tales of Patrick Creek: The River & Its Fish" (available at the ranger station) tells about this area, the spawning grounds for salmon and steelhead trout. If you are a fishing enthusiast, you know that salmon runs are from October through December and steelhead from December through April. With license and line in hand, follow the short access trail under the bridge to a barrier-free fishing platform. Good luck.

Across the highway and down a drive bordered by green lawns is Patrick Creek Lodge, its history dating back to the late nineteenth century as a way station on the stage route from the coast to Oregon. The current lodge, built in 1926, continues to provide lodging and fine dining year-round. Perhaps because I am usually a picnic person, I especially enjoyed the buffet lunch on the deck overlooking winding creekside paths and wee pools sheltered by huge old oaks.

The Smith River Scenic Byway portion of Highway 199 continues another five miles beyond Patrick Creek to the Randolph Collier Tunnel. The roadside rest stop on the north side, with bulletin boards picturing all the wonders to be found, is a perfect place to end (or begin) your journey.

Does the byway do justice to the man it honors? It is a brilliant span of engineering, forging through a rough, craggy land. It permits no crooked terrain to stop its course, no boulders too huge to halt its passage. Nor did Jedediah Smith. Would he have been astonished that a river carries his moniker? No way. After all, he named a longer, more important river for himself. Then an upstart, treader-on-his-heels changed it to the Trinity River—in the mistaken belief that it was the waterway to the Pacific, draining into the ocean at Trinidad Bay.

TRINITY RIVER SCENIC BYWAY

Chapter III
TRINITY RIVER SCENIC BYWAY
California State Highway 299
140 miles

It seems fitting for this scenic byway to begin in Shasta State Historic Park, its name changing from Reading Springs in 1848 to Shasta City a year later when the hamlet became the governmental center of Shasta County. Whether Major Pierson Barton Reading established the settlement after he discovered gold in nearby canyons, or whether it simply sprouted at the base of year-round springs, is a moot point. The site provided pure water and abundant trees to shelter the hundreds of glitter seekers who followed in Reading's wake.

As a newly arrived emigrant to California in the 1840s, Reading worked as a miner for John Sutter in the Sierra Mountains, served under Colonel John Fremont during the Mexican War, and acquired a 22,000-acre land grant along the upper Sacramento River. Convinced that there must be gold in the hills surrounding his rancho, Reading set out on the search in the spring of 1848. Making note of his adventure, he wrote: *My party consisted of 3 white men, one Delaware, one Chinook and about sixty Indians from the Sacramento Valley. I had 120 head of cattle with an abundant supply of provisions.* This crew served him well, scooping more than $80,000 worth of treasure from tributaries of the Trinity River.

When news of the strike spread south, zealous would-be-rich prospectors swarmed north-by-west, with Shasta City serving as the hub for all trails leading into the Trinities. Supplies for hungry (and thirsty) miners were carried by wagon train up the Sacramento River Valley and hauled into the mountains on muleback; mules that turned around and hauled over $2,000,000 worth of gold out of the mountains. At an estimated $20 an ounce in the early 1850s, that's a lot of nuggets!

SHASTA STATE HISTORIC PARK

The history of Shasta City reads like that of every shanty town in California during the gold-rush days. By 1849, log cabins had replaced miners' tents and, a year later, a sawmill supplied lumber for mercantiles, two hotels, and the wood-frame houses that bordered both sides of Main Street. In December of 1852, and again the following June, fire destroyed the whole shebang. With grim determination, enterprising citizens rebuilt the town within two years, constructing 28 brick-walled, iron-shuttered fireproof structures.

Several events toppled the throne of the Queen City of the Northern Diggings: in 1858, a wagon road was constructed over Buckhorn Pass between Redding and Weaverville; in 1868, the stage road from Shasta through French Gulch and over Scott Mountain to Oregon was shifted to an easier route up the Sacramento River Valley, and finally, in 1871, the Central Pacific Railroad, running up the valley, terminated its tracks at Poverty Flats instead of Shasta City. In 1888, when the county seat was moved to Poverty Flats (renamed Redding), Shasta City was doomed.

Many of the city's buildings that had replaced fire-destroyed edifices were torn down to supply bricks for the flourishing new town. It wasn't until 1922 that a preservation movement began to revive Old Shasta and, in 1937, the State of California acquired the property for an historic park. The museum housed in the courthouse is a good place to begin your exploration. Pick up a walking-tour brochure that provides complete information about the remaining structures, visit the jail downstairs, note the gallows in the backyard—and head out.

If possible, try to time your walk among the ruins for early morning or late afternoon when the jagged edges of crumbling bricks cast shadows on the pathway. Sense the mystic aura of shopkeepers, bartenders, hotel clerks and dance-hall girls, rough draymen and tough miners. Listen for the ghost voices in a variety of languages and dialects: Irish, Spanish, German and Chinese. Feel the magnetism of the thriving community that existed in the glory days: five hotels and five stage companies, a livery stable and blacksmith shop, a public bath-house and numerous saloons. And, as you leave this haunted place, be thankful that some of it has been preserved to remind us of our past.

As you leave Shasta City, be prepared to make a left turn at the top of Shasta Divide for a stop at Whiskeytown Lake. The visitor center for this National Recreation Area offers information about interpretive programs presented by the National Park Service, an orientation map, and brochures for self-guided tours around the lake. The park provides picnic areas, swimming beaches, boat launch ramps, marinas, and campgrounds—for a fee.

From the scenic overlook, over 40,000 acres of sky-reflecting blue water cover the canyon below. Created to supply power and irrigation for California's central valley, this enormous project was formed by diverting creeks flowing from the Trinity Mountains through a series of dams and tunnels. Completed in 1963, it is commemorated by a monument and plaque at the east end of the dam on Kennedy Memorial Drive, 1.5 miles from the visitor center. There you can listen to a recording of excerpts from President John F. Kennedy's dedication speech.

The drive around the lake heading west is delightful, especially midweek, spring or fall when summertime crowds have retreated to the cities. After traveling about six miles, turn right up the steep-sided gully of Trinity Mountain Road to French Gulch. A few stone buildings, neat wooden houses, and the charming, balconied French Gulch Hotel are all that remain to remind you of the boom days. Founded by French-Canadians, it proved to be the most productive placer mining district of the Northern California mines—to the tune of more than $50 million in gold.

There is a rumor that an infamous robber lifted some of that gold from a Wells Fargo stage. When Charles Bolton, alias Black Bart, was captured in 1883 after 27 robberies, the stage company published a list of his accomplishments. Among them was a holdup on September 1, 1880, on the Redding to Weaverville route—so the rumor is entirely possible. Black Bart has been remembered as a gentlemanly robber, never demanding money or jewels from the ladies, and for leaving hand-scrawled poems in place of the treasure boxes. A typical ending reads:

> *I've labored long and hard for bread—*
> *For honor and for riches.*
> *But on my corns too long you've tred,*
> *You fair-haired sons of bitches.*
> Black Bart, the PO8

Just past this junction, the byway leaves the lake and winds up in 20 miles-per-hour corkscrew curves for eight miles (with four passing lanes) to Buckhorn Summit (elevation 3213 ft.), the boundary line between Shasta and Trinity counties. This route follows the original toll road built by William Lowden in 1858, with rates of two cents a mile for one horseman, four cents per mile for a horse and buggy, and twenty cents a mile for a four-horse passenger wagon.

In the fall of 1862, William Brewer, a geologist hired to survey a road west, bounced over the summit on muleback. Of his perilous adventure, he wrote: *Trinity County is too rough to survey, all broken into rugged mountains and broken canyons thousands of feet deep with sides very steep and rocky.*

As you smoothly swing down into the valley below, consider the jolting trip stagecoach travelers endured during the last decades of the nineteenth century. It wasn't until 1923 that Highway 299 was completed to the coast. After mounting three more summits, twisting around innumerable curves, dodging jutting walls of rock and skirting precarious steep-sided canyons, you will appreciate the road builders' back-breaking efforts. Those road-cuts are a geologist's dreamscape. If I haven't completely discouraged you from venturing farther—mush on.

You will soon understand why this curling ribbon of road achieved scenic byway status 70 years after its completion. Not only does it drift through an incredibly beautiful stretch of landscape, it also transports you from the dry manzanita and black oak chaparral country of the inland valleys and along Ponderosa, big leaf maple, and California buckeye riverside terrain, it also leads you up to the heights of Douglas fir and sugar pine forests.

About 20 miles from Buckhorn Summit, the Trinity River suddenly appears in view. Although two dams in the mountains control its normally turbulent flow, to paraphrase Mark Twain's description of the Mississippi, *The Trinity is worth considering.* As you trace its course, you will observe its ever-changing character: crystalline and foaming buoyantly with the onrush of snowmelt in the spring, or murky and sluggishly indolent, barely burbling along at the end of summer.

If you are tempted to test its waters, watch for Indian Creek Lodge on your right, a small motel with spacious lawns, shade trees, and nine acres of river frontage. This is an especially calm section of river, ideal for fishing, swimming, easy rafting or tubing. You might even try your luck at gold panning.

A mile and a half past the motel, cross the bridge over the river and turn left on Steiner Flat Road into Douglas City. Originally dubbed Kanaka Bar, its name was changed to honor Stephen A. Douglas after he won a seat in the U.S. Senate, defeating Abraham Lincoln. (I wonder if the new senator ever knew of the honor bestowed on him?) Drive past the general store and continue a half mile up a steep hill and down a steep hill into a BLM (Bureau of Land Management) campground. At the bottom of the grade is a bronze tablet set into a boulder commemorating Reading's Bar, where Major Reading made his first gold strike. The campground is heavily wooded, providing pleasant camping sites and a large turnaround paved parking area with a trail leading down to the river—an ideal spot for fisherfolk.

When you return to Highway 299, proceed west and pull into the spacious reststop on the left. There is plenty of parking, (even for large RVs or cars with trailers), picnic tables in the shade, restrooms, and bulletin boards displaying information about the area. You will learn that this wayside honors Moon Lim Lee, the man who gave the Chinese Joss House in Weaverville to the State of California.

At this point, the highway leaves the Trinity River for 15 miles. It does, however, cross Weaver Creek and traces it north seven miles to Weaverville, a five-diamond village in a 24 karat setting. It is said this enclave, nestled amidst mountains, incredibly green in the summer and white mantled in winter, provided the inspiration for Shangri-la in James Hilton's *Lost Horizons*. (The Ojai Valley in Southern California, however, was chosen as the setting for the 1937 film by Frank Capra.) The byway widens to four lanes, accommodating the Trinity Plaza shopping center, automotive shops, and a sawmill, then narrows again as it approaches the old town, listed on the National Register of Historic Places.

Every traveler probably has a different approach to reconnoitering an unknown town. Mine is to slowly drive through, come about, park midway, and explore by *shank's mare* on foot. With a place as small as Weaverville

Weaverville

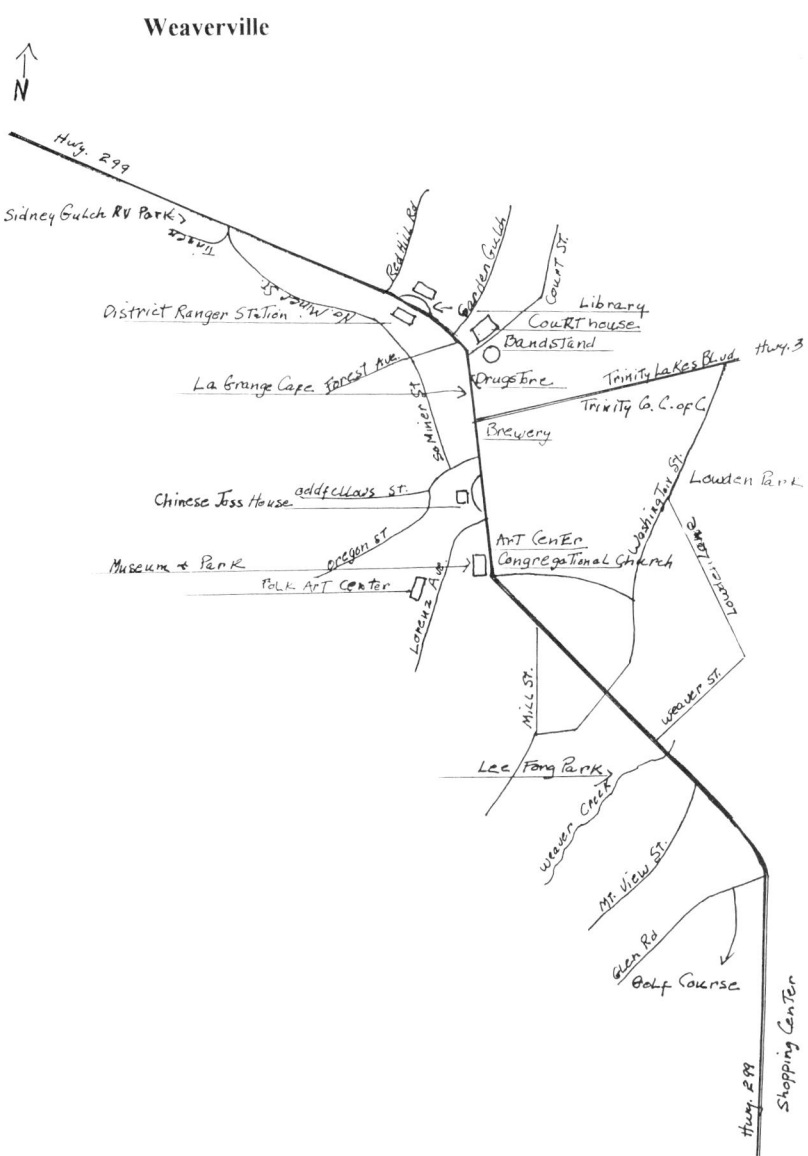

(population 3000), this is feasible. Rather than simply listing must-see-sights, I'd like to take you on a walkabout with me. It will soon become obvious that this community takes great pride in its heritage

During the many days I devoted to this fascinating village, it became my habit to park under venerable old locust trees in front of the Congregational Church, built in 1891 and impeccably maintained. Your attention will immediately be caught by the gabled, white-frame house next door, built in 1893 as the first parsonage. Fronted by green lawns, colorful borders of petunias, and a picket fence, it is now the Highland Art Center. Visitors are welcomed by a receptionist and encouraged to wander through the spacious galleries exhibiting the work of regional artists. Studios of resident painters, potters, weavers, and photographers are housed within the main complex and around the grounds in former barns and woodsheds. Definitely worth a visit, whether you are an art aficionado or not.

As you walk up Main Street, you will sense a town fairly bursting with energy, old fashioned friendliness and common courtesy. After passing a gift shop in a rammed-earth adobe building that once housed a mortuary, you will see the old brick Pacific Brewery building, now occupied by the Red Dragon restaurant. It seems appropriate for Chinese decor to replace western memorabilia and beer kegs, since this end of Weaverville was once Chinatown.

Crossing Trinity Lakes Blvd., past the New York Hotel (official stage stop in the 1880s) and the renovated New York Saloon (California's second oldest existing historical saloon), you will see Weaverville's most photographed spectacle—outside spiral staircases from the sidewalks to overhanging balconies. The original buildings, constructed wall-to-wall, had two owners, one on the lower floor and another on the upper, necessitating stairways on the outside. You might want to stop underneath the first one to visit the Weaverville Drug Store, the oldest pharmacy in the state. Advertisements inform us it is *owned by two Hicks*, Frank E. Hicks, Jr. and Patricia J. Hicks, the town historian. They have preserved the antique apothecary decor, as well as dispensing the usual drugstore paraphernalia.

On the corner of Main and Court streets you will pass a 1910 bandstand and cross the street to one of the oldest courthouses in the state. Built in 1856 as a store, office building, and hotel, it was purchased by Trinity County in 1865 for $9000. Watch carefully for traffic along Highway 299 (no traffic lights in this town), then cross the main drag to visit Hays Book Store. The many little nooks contain a fine array of local history and lore, current best-sellers, and books on tape, maps, magazines, greeting cards and postcards, and a special section just for children.

Heading back south along the west side of Main Street, you can pop into two adjacent old buildings that once housed a hardware and general merchandise store, now remodeled as Courthouse Square, a series of small shops. Stop in the office of *The Trinity Journal* to pick up a newspaper and a copy of the *Trinity County Recreation Guide*. Down in the middle of the block, you will pass under the second spiral staircase and pay can a visit to Greg Olson's Stoneware Shop, a collection of locally produced pottery. Next to it is La Grange Cafe, a casual bar-lunch room, with a more formal room for fine dining. "The best place in town to eat"—according to locals.

WEAVERVILLE

Opposite the intersection of Highway 3 and down a smidgen was the location of Chinatown, a smattering of tiny shacks completely destroyed in the fire of 1905. Across Oregon Street is the *Temple of the Forest Beneath the Clouds*, built in 1874 by Chinese who placer-mined the gold diggings of Trinity County. Although still used for worship, the Joss House became a part of California's State Park system in 1956 through the efforts of Moon Lim Lee, a descendant of one of the builders. The simple wood-frame structure contains intricately carved, ornate artifacts, colorful brocade banners, and painted figures of Chinese deities.

After a short walk south, you can roam through the huge, brick-walled exhibit hall of the Jackson Memorial Museum. Under the auspices of the Trinity County Historical Society, the museum displays native artifacts and a collection of ranching and gold mining equipment; an extensive array of firearms and fossils; old bottles, chinaware, kitchen utensils, and furniture used by the first settlers. A smaller room housing the History Center Archives, containing documents, and court and county records, is open to the public for research.

An adjacent outdoor historic park features a blacksmith's shop and a steam-powered stampmill, designed to extract gold from ore. A 13 by 20 feet woodplanked cabin, made of ax-hewn boards with dovetail joints, removed from the La Grange Mine, once provided housing for a ditch tender. This structure is the only one surviving of those placed at five-mile intervals along a 29 mile-long waterway during the 1850s.

On the west end of town, you can catch your breath and catch up on the news in the Trinity County Library. A circular driveway permits easy access and parking. Across the highway, drop into the district ranger station for complete information about hiking and camping in the Shasta-Trinity National Forest.

Weaverville's thoughtfully preserved historic buildings defy the image of this dignified village as an outpost of debauchery. Its beginning reads like a script for a Wild West show. The hamlet was founded by three miners, who decided to toss a coin and name it after one of them. John Weaver was the winner of the coin toss. Several small camps formed the first township, revealing the origins of its settlers: French and English Town, German and

Irish Town, and Faggtown, named for Robert Fagg, an early miner. The village grew to accommodate four gambling houses and 14 saloons, 1500 gold miners and a few women of ill repute.

It was not until some 30 respectable ladies arrived on the scene that a church and schoolhouse were built, balls replaced brawls, and parades and theatrical events replaced shoot-outs. Today, Weaverville honors its heritage in a continuation of these festivals: Chinese New Year, arts and crafts exhibits, a major 4th of July celebration, a summer-long series of concerts, and small theater productions.

After your sojourn in Weaverville, and as you continue westward, the destructive effects of the fire during the summer of 2001 become apparent. Although the forest service has replanted the area with seedlings, it will be years before groves of pine once more cloak the hillsides.

The highway climbs to an elevation of 2897 feet at Oregon Mountain Summit, providing a stunning view of Weaver Bally Peak (elev. 7504 ft.). On the left side of Highway 299, an interpretive stop describes the history of the La Grange Mine, a California registered historical landmark. Beginning operation in Oregon Gulch in 1851, it was purchased by the La Grange Hydraulic Gold Mining Company in 1892. The huge *monitor*, used for blowing hillsides into bits of gravel through streams of water spouting from its nozzle, is permanently mounted by the roadside. As water for washing the gravel in Weaver Creek dwindled, water was brought from Stuart Fork River through 29 miles of ditches, tunnels, and flumes. Downriver, you will see the results: hillsides denuded of all vegetation, gullies stripped bare to bedrock, and beaches piled high with tailings. When the golden treasure gave out, the hydraulic equipment was used to carve out the highway, as if a giant mole had burrowed through the mountaintop.

From the summit, the road winds downhill to Canyon Creek, flowing into the Trinity River at Junction City. Once bustling with prospectors, floods washed away the original buildings and fires destroyed many of the rebuilt structures. (A familiar story all over the West.) An 1860s schoolhouse and the sagging Junction City Hotel are the only remnants.

Canyon Creek Road, a riot of flower-filled crevices in the spring, is paved for 13 miles and leads up to the Trinity Alps trailhead. It has become such a popular access for the boot and backpack crowd, that there is now a quota system for its use. Permits can be acquired at the ranger station on the south side of the highway.

A few miles farther, turn right onto a side road for a quick look at Helena, once a thriving trading post. Settled by two German families, they operated a pack-train business, a hotel for wayfarers, and a brewery, now only a brick shell entangled by blackberry bushes. The townsite is a private property and trespassing is not permitted.

For the next 50 miles, Trinity River Scenic Byway lives up to its name, closely tracking the water's edge or riding high above. As you drive downriver, try to visualize the great flood during the winter of 1861-1862. Measured at 47 feet above previous high-water marks, everything in its path was swept away: bridges, roads, buildings, and dams, leaving behind broken tree stumps and tons of flow-clogging debris. You will get a glimpse of the river's power at the confluence of the North Fork branch with the main Trinity River. Here the water churns violently over and around boulders—serious white-water riffles. The names given to the rapids are self-explanatory: Hell's Hole, The Slot, Zigzag, and Fishtail. In Big Flat you will see advertisements for rafting and kayaking instructions and river-running guided adventures. For the less intrepid, and families with small children, runs are made in more placid waters from Big Flat to Big Bar, another hangout for river-runners.

Incidentally, the addition of *Bar* to village names along the river does not denote a drinking establishment (although they are a part of the scene) but refers to a ridge of sand gravel above the surface of the water, sometimes yielding gold. All of this is explained by exhibits at Big Bar Ranger Station on the north side of the highway. Built during the early 1900s, the station occupies a strategic spot midway along the byway. To add to your enjoyment of the next stop, be sure to pick up the pamphlet, *"Wildlife of the Trinity River."*

Four miles from Big Bar is White's Bar, a cool respite on a hot summer's day with picnic tables shaded by white alder and leafy-green willows. It is also a sanctuary for tropical birds flying north from their winter sojourn and a forest service banding station. As you quietly walk the riverbanks, you'll be entranced by the song-and-dance breeding ritual, the yellow warbler's high-pitched trill, or the eke of a black-headed grosbeak. You'll thankfully watch swallows diving on annoying mosquitoes, and you might spot an American dipper or water ouzel bobbing its way under the waves in search of other insects.

TREE SWALLOW   CALIFORNIA DIPPER

Thirteen miles farther west, Cedar Flat is another information access point, this one describing the Chirmariko Indians. These earliest inhabitants along a 20-mile stretch of the Trinity River from Big Bar to the South Fork of the Trinity were of Hokan stock. One of the smallest distinct tribes in the Western states, with an estimated population of 250 in 1849, it is now extinct.

Another mile west, after crossing the river, you pass Burnt Ranch, its name applied after the settlement was destroyed by the natives. Between this small burg and Hawkins Bar, the road rides high above an abyss. A scenic overlook permits an osprey's view of a ridge of rocks projecting over boulder-strewn rapids far below. At this point, the Trinity is joined by the New River, rushing through a terrain so pristine, that 21 miles of it became a part of the National Wild and Scenic River system in 1980.

A narrow, twisting road leads into this isolated country and, after 18 miles, to the infamous community of Denny, its questionable reputation due to the dangers posed by marijuana growers' objections to interlopers. (Apparently, recent efforts to curb this activity have been successful.) Long before backpackers and pot-growers invaded the territory, an offshoot of the Shasta Indians, termed New River Shasta by ethnologists, somehow managed to exist among the extremely rugged, alpine mountaintops. They are now another extinct band of natives.

The drive becomes easier after passing the reststop on the south side of the highway and crossing the bridge into Salyer. A tiny wayside chapel built in 1923 still invites the faithful to worship on Sunday. A mile farther downriver, the Trinity is joined by the South Fork branch, flowing some 60 miles or more from the Yolla Bolly Wilderness. The junction now serves as the border between Trinity and Humboldt counties.

Although the river turns to flow north from Highway 299, the Trinity River Scenic Byway continues through Willow Creek and west on Highway 299 some 32 miles to Blue Lake. It's an easy drive with many passing lanes. A vista point atop Berry Summit (elev. 2659 ft.) offers splendid views of Redwood Creek Valley, its headwaters in the mountains to the south. The sight of thickly forested mountains and naked, clear-cut slopes will both please and offend you.

The next high point, Lord Ellis Summit (elev. 2262 ft.) was not named for English nobility but for two men who were responsible for an improved pack-train trail that provided easier access for sheep ranchers living in the valleys below. These summits mark the western edge of the Klamath Mountains and the east end of the Coast Range.

The highway drops down into the Mad River Valley and a left turn will take you into the little community of Blue Lake, with no visible view of a lake. It began as a timbertown and a freight loading and pack-mule station for miners heading east into the gold country. In 1854, a short 7.5 mile rail line was built into town from the coast.

The old Arcata-Mad River depot on Railroad Avenue, a California Historical Landmark, is now a museum dedicated to preserving the history of the railroad, logging, and timber operations. Blue Lake is also known for the Mad River Festival, with performances given on weekends every summer by the Dell' Arte Players Company, and as the Gateway into the Klamath-Trinity Country.

It should be quite obvious to readers of this guide that you can, indeed, begin your journey on the Trinity River Scenic Byway by turning east out of Arcata onto Highway 299. You might be glad to leave the fast-paced traffic of Highway 101, rushing north along the Pacific Coast, to leisurely wander through an equally beautiful landscape to the west.

BIGFOOT SCENIC BYWAY

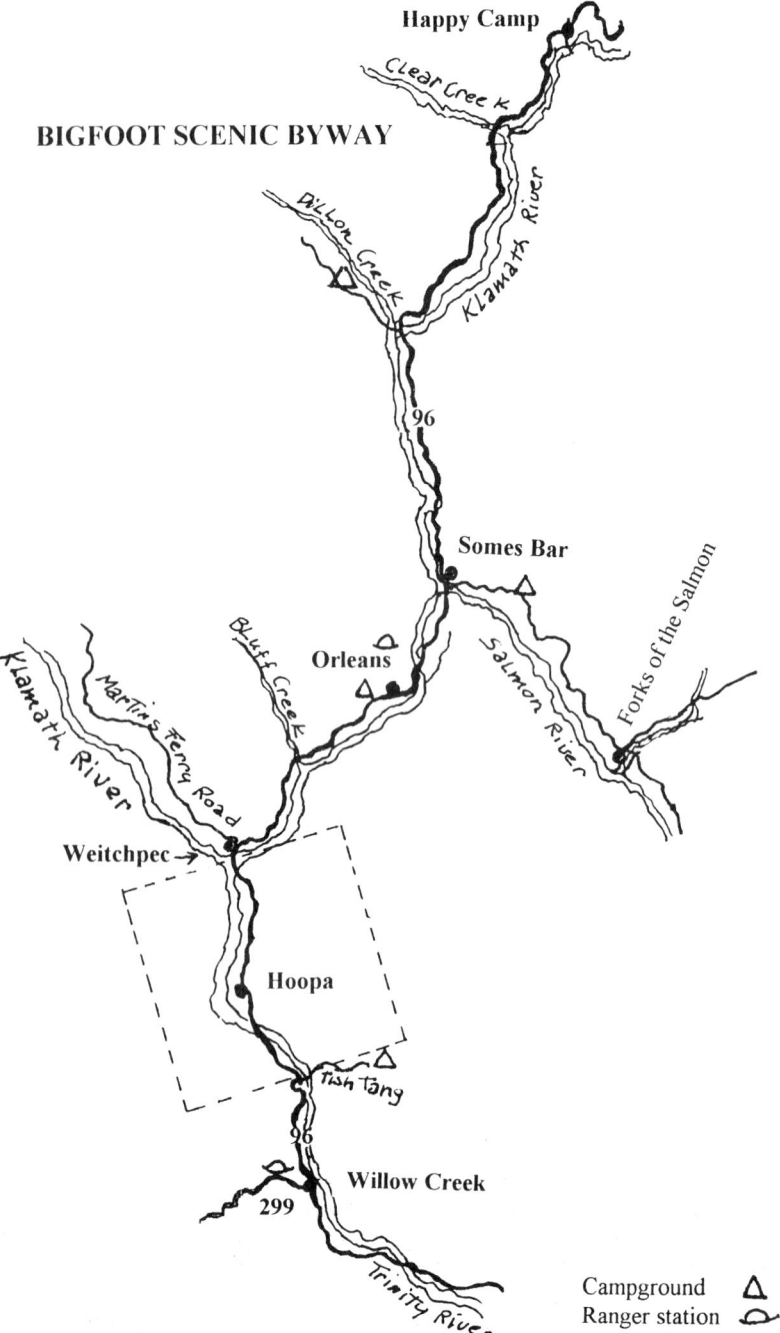

Chapter IV
BIGFOOT SCENIC BYWAY
California State Highway 96
88 Miles

It is about time this elusive creature received the recognition and respect he (or she) so rightly deserves. Never harming anyone, the human/beast is not something to fear but to admire. There certainly has been enough research to offset the notoriety of its dubious reputation and to silence skepticism about its survival. However, does the dedication of the Bigfoot Scenic Byway on April Fools' Day, 2001, suggest that some ambiguity still exists?

As *Gateway to Bigfoot Country* the town of Willow Creek epitomizes its slogan. To validate the community's commitment, the local newspaper, *The Kourier*, carries the byline "Bigfoot Capital of the World." On Labor Day weekends, the town's superstar is honored by Bigfoot Days, including a parade; softball, golf and cribbage tournaments; a pancake breakfast and an old-fashioned ice-cream social. Various business establishments, a motel, the golf club, and Bigfoot Rafting Company proudly flaunt the moniker.

Even the Willow Creek-China Flat Museum has added a Bigfoot wing to its complex. You can't miss the massive sculpture, strangely adorned with hair of featherlike carvings, standing guard in front of the building. Inside you will find evidential materials accumulated by Bob Titus, investigator/taxidermist, who donated his collection to the museum. Within a well-organized research center are videotapes, books, magazine articles, newspaper stories, accounts of sightings, and drawers filled with plaster casts of foot and hand prints.

The main museum building displays equally interesting artifacts detailing the history of China Flat, an 1850s settlement of Chinese miners on the lower Trinity River. Glass-covered (and locked) cases of gold nuggets attest to their success. Several other rooms display remnants of the once flourishing timber trade and memorabilia of Willow

Willow Creek

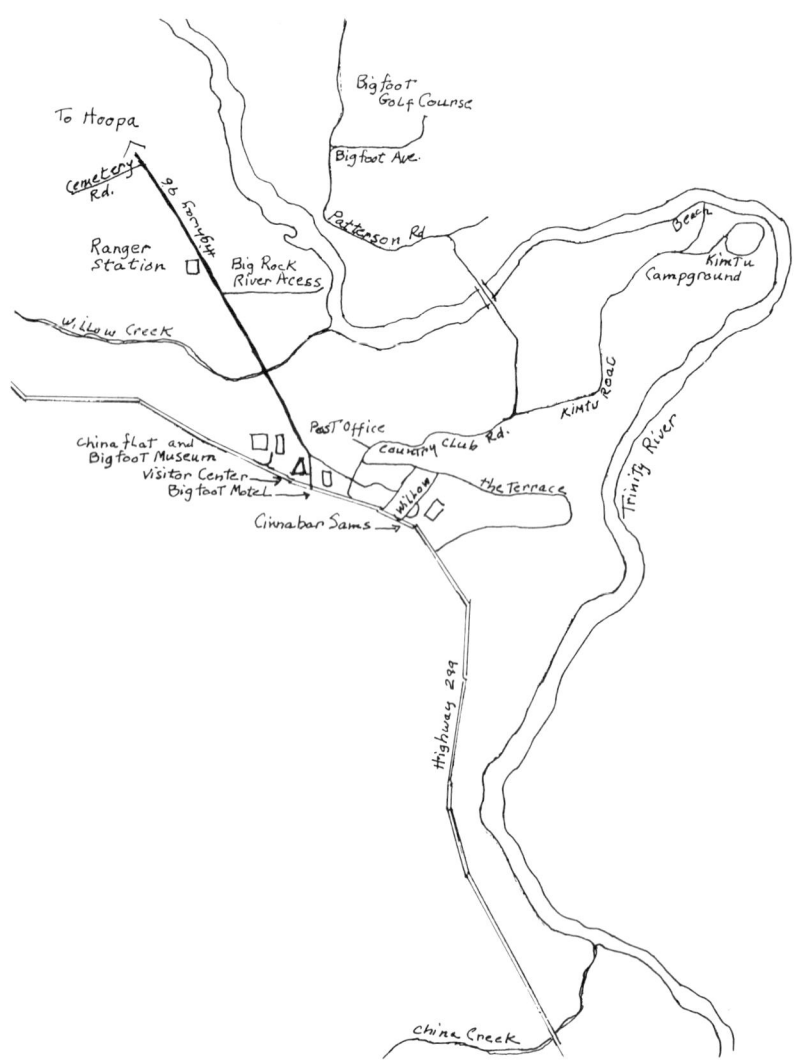

Creek's first families. Located on the border of Trinity and Humboldt counties, and distantly removed from both county seats, the town was sort of an outpost, a way station between the inland valleys and the coast. Yet, its strategic location at the junction of two branches of the Trinity River fostered its role as supply center for miners, loggers, and settlers.

Today, taking full advantage of the river and enclosed by the Six Rivers National Forest, Willow Creek also perfectly epitomizes its other slogan, *River Fun in the Mountain Sun.* With the Trinity winding sinuously through the valley, vacationers swim off its beaches, fish along its banks, kayak in its waters, and pan for gold in its gravel. Rafters run rapids and inner-tubers drift, campers pitch tents, and trekkers hike trails. Birders list rare species, naturalists photograph wildlife, and anthropologists still roam the forests in search of Bigfoot.

Conveniently situated at the intersection of Highways 299 and 96, the tourist information office is enhanced by its own more realistic sculpture of Bigfoot. A bronze plaque in front of the statue honors Don Cave, who spearheaded the effort by Willow Creek Community Services to purchase the property from CalTrans. The volunteer receptionist can tell you about local events and small theater productions, and provide a map and brochures highlighting area attractions. (A nice addition to small-town ambiance is the public restroom in a concrete building in back.)

Unlike Weaverville, flaunting its renovated bits of nineteenth-century architecture, Willow Creek seems fresh and new, sparkling in its simplicity. Its downtown may be tiny—a one-mile stretch along Highway 299—but there's nothing shabby about this place. It is one of the first California rural towns to be designated the recipient of a beautification grant for new sidewalks and extensive landscaping.

The first time I visited Willow Creek and inquired about a good place for lunch, I was directed to Cinnabar Sam's. I've returned on every visit for breakfast, lunch, or dinner. The rustic yet elegant wood-frame building, with several dining levels and an outdoor deck, was designed by owner Steve Paine to house his immense collection of Western treasures. Big-game heads, with signs naming the hunters, are mounted below the rafters, and the walls are covered with posters and paintings of the olden days. The menu is as eclectic as the decor, offering Miner's Primers, such as Hobo Potato Skins and Crusty Zuckies, and Macho Man's Fare like Bareback Buckin' Beef Dip and Pony Butte's BBQ Ribs. When I asked Steve how he chose the name for his restaurant, he handed me a printout telling the story (fact or fancy?) and showed me a painting of Sam himself, who bore a remarkable resemblance to Mark Twain. It hangs on the wall across from his office door. Wandering through this incredible establishment is even better than visiting a museum—and more fun.

Willow Creek's setting in this forest-bordered river valley invites you to stay awhile and explore. It will be well worth your time to tour the area and see what interesting and unusual possibilities are available. Drive north on Country Club Road (Chevron Station on the corner) past the post office and *The Kourier* office. After one-half mile, at the Y intersection, head to the right for the Kimtu Recreation Area. You will soon pass Veterans Park, complete with ball field, tennis courts, picnic tables, and restrooms. Stop in the children's playground to see the bronze plaque placed by the Boy Scouts, honoring Jedediah Smith who "camped here May 6, 1828." The road continues down to a river access point, swimming beach, and a community operated campground, with an attendant in charge. Future site for an RV park with hookups? Or my wishful thinking?

Return to the intersection, turn right and cross the bridge over the river, turn left on Patterson Road and continue to Bigfoot Country Club. The golf course is a beautifully laid out nine-hole, par-35 course, meandering around ponds and through stands of stately evergreens and drooping willow trees. If you drive the streets winding over the hills beyond, you will see elegant homes shaded by ancient oaks and enclosed by split-rail fences bordering acres of lavish green lawns.

Before you leave town to head north on Bigfoot Scenic Byway, be sure to fuel up. Gas stations are scarce on Highway 96. Drop into the district ranger station (west side) to gather information on recreation in the Six Rivers National Forest, day-use picnic areas, and camping spots. If you are a camper, be sure to ask which campgrounds are open; some have been closed due to federal cutbacks in funding. Across from the station, behind the gravel min-

ing operation, is Big Rock, a river beach open to the public for fishing, boating, and swimming.

As soon as you leave busy Highway 299, it's as if you've entered another world and stepped back to a simpler way of life; traffic is sparse and towns are few and far between. The meadows where gold miners once pitched their tents are now planted with vineyards, and on the hillsides, once stripped bare of timber, fruit orchards thrive. With most of the acreage surrounding Willow Creek privately owned by farmers, it appears the town won't be cluttered with urban sprawl in the near future. If you are traveling this route during the summer months, I suggest a stop at the red-barn produce stand of the Trinity River Farm to buy fresh fruits and vegetables for a snack to tide you over between cafes.

After offering occasional glimpses of the river through the oak-tree-bordered highway, the road rises high above its banks, and becomes narrow and twisting, with steep drop-offs on the right-hand side. Not to worry. There are several photo-opportunity pullouts along the brink. Near the top of the grade, a large billboard on the right directs your attention to Tish-Tang Campground. The Indian name means *neck of land projecting into the river*. Along the paved road leading down to the shaded campsites is a mural of forest creatures and native plants painted on the concrete retaining wall.

Immediately beyond is another colorful sign, Welcome to Hoopa, where a vista point affords a splendid view of California's largest Indian reservation, 144-square miles. Although the designation for the tribe and the valley is spelled Hoopa, the people are referred to as the Hupas.

The Hoopa Tribal Council is the governing body of the entire valley, maintaining control over all of its affairs, providing a wide range of services and protection to its people. Municipal functions include ambulance service and a radio station; health, education, and social services; a judicial system and court; police and legal departments. The tribe owns and operates several business enterprises: a fish hatchery, which plants salmon and steelhead fingerlings in the river; the Hoopa Forest Industry, a timber harvesting company; and the Hoopa Valley Shopping Center.

Located within the center is a well-stocked market, a ubiquitous casino full of slot machines, and (a bit more upscale) the Hoopa Tribal Museum. You will see a wonderful collection of finely-woven baskets, ceremonial regalia, dugout canoes, and tools used by the NaTiniXwe people (na-tin-o-whey, *where the trails return*.)

Although visitors are welcome on the reservation, you should remember these are not public lands but are privately owned by tribal members. Tours to reconstructed village sites, with information about the building of houses and sweat lodges, can be arranged through the museum or at the tribal office. If you are especially energetic, you can participate in a unique program organized by the tribe to give visitors an understanding of the work of field biologists. This is a workday, not a field trip for tourists, and might include a spotted owl survey, banding songbirds, or counting the fish harvest.

For more information about the history of the Hoopa Valley Indian Reservation and its ceremonial celebrations, local fishing and rafting guide services, hiking trails, and backcountry scenic drives, the recently published book *In Hoopa Territory* is listed in the bibliography.

As Highway 96 leaves the valley and leads north, the road again winds high above a boulder-strewn gorge cut through the hills by the Trinity. About 3.5 miles from the Hoopa Valley Shopping Center, there is a large gravel turnout affording a view of the river, 100 steep feet below—not a great view for acrophobics. After another six miles, the Hoopa Reservation ends at Weitchpec, where the Trinity melds with the Klamath River and turns abruptly to flow northwest to the Pacific.

The confluence was once the site of three Yurok villages, but today their reservation stretches along the 40-mile narrow, rocky Klamath River canyon—and therein lies a major dispute. For centuries, the Yuroks and the Hupas roamed freely along the rivers and among the mountains, sharing salmon runs and harvesting timber. Then in the 1850s, the rush for gold brought hordes of miners into their territory. After the devastation left from a boom gone bust, surviving tribal members were gathered by the U. S. government to sign the treaty of October 5, 1851, and the military post of Fort Gaston was established to maintain order. After another decade, the Superintendent of Indian Affairs designated the entire 12-mile-square valley, and the extension along the Klamath, as the Hoopa Reservation, to be shared with the Yuroks.

However, in 1988, Congress passed an act granting the Hupas exclusive right to the valley watered by the Trinity, including revenue derived from the timber harvest. The Yuroks were given the unproductive strip along the Klamath. Only a 15-mile stretch of Highway 169 follows the river downstream from Weitchpec, with no connection to its western terminus at Klamath Glen, five miles from Highway 101. (Ah, the vagaries of politics!)

I've only driven downriver for three miles to the point where John Martin operated a ferry and way station for pack trains coming from the coast from 1858 to 1875. Even though now paved, I thought with compassion about Jedediah Smith's struggles as he wrote in his journal: *Crossing a deep rocky ravine, I found greater obstacles than I had before encountered.*

Today at Weitchpec, "home of tackle bustin' steelhead and salmon," fisherfolk buy flies, locals buy supplies, and travelers can buy gas at Pearson's Grocery (left-hand side of Highway 96). A dirt trail behind the store leads down to a riverbar, access for fishing and rafting. Walk across the bridge above the junction of the two rivers and imagine, if you will, the torrential rains of 1964, when all towns along the rivers were completely cut off. Raging waters wiped out bridges, felled trees to clog the streams with debris, and covered all roads with several feet of gravel. Natural forces don't treat this mountainous terrain lightly.

From the confluence of the Trinity and Klamath rivers, the drive northeast upstream along the Klamath is spectacular, with a viewpoint turnout three miles from Weitchpec. When the highway enters Six Rivers National Forest, a half mile beyond, the terrain is not so steep and there are numerous access trails down to the river. Although the forest service campground at Aiken's Creek may be closed, as it was during my many drives along Highway 96, I suggest pulling into the wide, flat parking area and taking a leg-stretching stroll along the riverbank.

Immediately beyond, you will pass an abandoned building, Bluff Creek Company Store, and a has-seen-better-days trailer park. After another mile, a bridge crosses Bluff Creek, with a scenic pullout overlooking the junction of the creek with the river. A road on the left leads up into the backcountry, where in 1958 traces of Bigfoot were first noted by a native tractor driver working on a logging trail. Thereafter, researchers have frequently gathered along Bluff Creek, making casts of gigantic footprints imprinted into the sandy bar. This is the area where, on October 20, 1967, photographer Roger Patterson shot the controversial film of a huge, hairy creature stalking through the woods, a location which was later verified by four other investigators.

After riding high above the Klamath, the highway again slopes down to water level. Across the river can be seen cultivated fields and organic farms, orchards and vineyards, bursts of vivid green and deep purple against rocky, gray cliffs. Then you come into Orleans, "the center of the world, in the middle of nowhere." I think of it as a throw-back place, reminiscent of its logging and mining years—yet no ghost town this, no wallowing in its historicness nor bustling with activity. It seems to say, slow down, relax, tarry awhile, and get to know us—and the

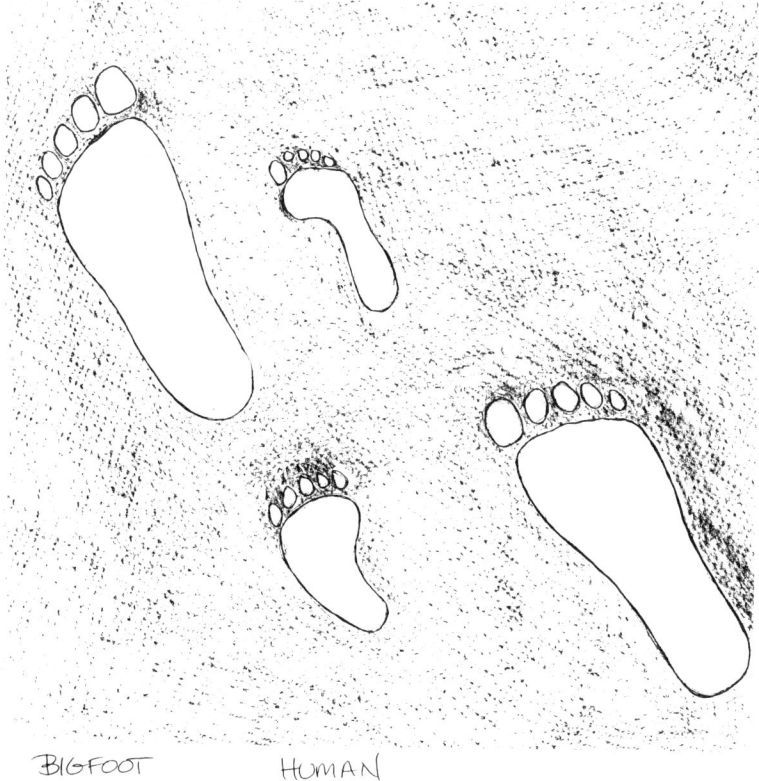

first place you pass on the right exemplifies this invitation.

Freshly mowed lawns stretch along the roadway, flags flap in the breeze, and colorful blooms encircle the sign Klamath Riverside RV Park. (This is my home-away-from-home when I'm in Orleans.) Even if you are not an RVer, drive in and say "hello" to Karen and Mark O'Rourke, who transformed a dilapidated fish camp into as elegant a campground as you will find anywhere. The amenities are numerous: shaded, grassy sites, nicely separated with rose bushes; immaculate showers and laundry room; a pavilion for potluck suppers; a playing field for children; a swimming pool and hot tub—and their very own Bigfoot statue. You might like to rent one of the on-site trailers to get a feel for the RV lifestyle, or sign up for a half-day guided rafting or drift-boat fishing trip, picnic lunch included. Recommended!

Across the way, a sprawling, slightly-ramshackle building, with a rowboat incongruously perched on its peak, will immediately catch your attention: The Orleans Mining Co. Mall: The last of the Mom and Pop Cafes. Wander through its tacked-on rooms to inspect old mining equipment and logging saws, the "world's largest" cast-iron pot and, hanging on the walls, a huge collection of iron skillets, with signatures and quaint sayings inscribed from visitors from all over the world. It's not a bad place to eat—in fact, the only place in town to eat! Miraculously appearing from a tiny kitchen are steak and eggs, biscuits and gravy, hamburgers, a huge chef's salad, and beer served in frosty mugs.

The Mall also includes a motel—the only motel in town—12 simple rooms with clean facilities and some kitchen stuff, plus a bunkhouse for hikers, river rafters, and fishermen. Air conditioning? There are swamp coolers on the roof for each building. (See what I meant by a throw-back place?) More information about this friendly village can be obtained from the Chamber of Commerce located in the Orleans Commercial Services District Office next to the RV park.

The settlement of New Orleans Bar dates its recorded beginning, as do most river towns around the Klamath Mountains, to the gold rush days of the mid 1800s. When California was admitted to the union in 1850, the vast northern territory below the Oregon border was divided into two counties, Shasta and Trinity. In 1851, Klamath County, with the county seat in Orleans, was created from a northern section of Trinity. In 1852, Siskiyou County was formed from portions of Shasta and Klamath and, five years later, Klamath was further whittled down by Del Norte, to be finally assimilated by Humboldt and Siskiyou counties.

The name applied to Orleans by the original inhabitants, the Karuks, was *panamnik* translated into the apt description of "white man's campground." Another source claims the name means "flat place" or "little valley." No nostalgic structures remain of the white man's occupation. The old hotel that once housed the young engineer Herbert Hoover was destroyed by fire in 2000. A stark rock chimney alongside empty cellar holes, back-dropped by green-mantled mountains and surrounded by a field of wildflowers, is all that remains. Plans are in progress to develop the site into an educational retreat for California schoolteachers, rebuilding the lodge in traditional Karuk redwood-plank style. Under the auspices of *Wild By Nature, Inc.*, classes will be offered in California history and environmental studies from an indigenous perspective, earning university credit. The organizers are working in collaboration with the Karuk Tribe, CIBA (California Indian Basketweavers Assoc.), CNPS (California Native Plant Society), and Humboldt and San Diego State universities. A bistro featuring local organic foods prepared by a Karuk gourmet chef will add another native touch to the project.

Also consumed by fire (but many years earlier than the hotel fire) was the first one-lane, wooden bridge spanning the Klamath River. Even the bridge built to replace the burned structure was swept away by the floodwaters of 1964. The new bridge, completed in 1966, is entirely constructed of steel and concrete and will surely survive any catastrophe devised by fickle Mother Nature.

Although still laid-back, the citizens of Orleans are edging their way into the twenty-first century and across the "digital divide." The Community Computer Center, begun in September 1999, provides free computer and Internet access for 300 registered users, as well as basic instruction by a staff of volunteers. While I was staying in Orleans, I was given permission (for a small donation) to check my e-mail messages on my computer at home.

The village seems to be a melding place for old-timers and the newly retired, for artisans and craftspeople, firefighters and road crews, gold panners and, intermittently, mushroom hunters. Pickers move south from Washington and Oregon in search of matsutake mushrooms. This highly prized edible fungi requires an exact recipe of rain, sun, and cold to grow in the mixed conifer-hardwood forests that carpet the northwestern states. Traveling in campers, pickup trucks, and trailers, a group of pickers will gather in a community such as Orleans and scour the mountainsides, sometimes harvesting under snow. Their finds are carefully cleaned with soft paint brushes (no water) and sold to buyers, who may pay as much as $89 per pound for number ones—the unformed buds. Number fives and sixes are generally rejected, as they are too mature to survive handling and air-shipping and still have a shelf life. The matsutakes are then trucked to SeaTac Airport in Seattle to be flown to Japan, where they are considered a special delicacy.

Located on the border of the Six Rivers and Klamath national forests, Orleans can also rightfully boast to being a focal point for the Klamath River region—and paradise for those who revel in sportfishing. It is to this prime country that Chinook salmon and steelhead (ocean going rainbow trout) annually fight their way from the ocean upriver to spawn, the run generally starting in August and continuing until early fall.

When Jedediah Smith turned west along the Klamath in 1828, he wrote: *There are so many salmon that you could walk across the river on their backs.* Alas, nearly two centuries later, commercial fishing and pollution from heavy logging and agricultural runoff have greatly reduced the number of salmon swimming upriver to spawn. Consequently, catch quotas and restrictions have been applied and the situation has improved. Inquire at the ranger station on Ishi Pishi Road for current regulations.

At this end of Orleans, you have a choice for continuing north. You can pass the ranger station and drive on the west side of the river, staying on Ishi Pishi Road, until you arrive at Somes Bar. Or you can stay on Highway 96 and continue north on the east side of the river.

If you leave Orleans via Highway 96, instead of driving the very narrow and windy back road, you will cross the Klamath on the new bridge and begin to climb above the valley. I like to linger awhile on a high point in one of the wide turnouts and watch hawks soar, ride a downdraft, and suddenly swoop to snatch their prey. Many of the turnouts have dirt trails that twist and turn down to the river, where men in waders go to net a fish.

Drive this route cautiously. The heavy rains of 1998 caused massive mudslides, leaving piles of rubble and wide gaps along the sides. At one point, a scrunchy, one-lane bridge with high metal gridlike sides covers a gaping hole. White-knuckle driving for this traveler, nudging the camper over the rattling span!

The highway soon crosses the border between Humboldt and Siskiyou counties at Somes Bar, a mere spot-in-the-road. It was originally settled by Abraham Somes in 1850 a couple miles up the Salmon River from its present location, where extremely steep mountain sides permitted only three hours of sun during the winter. In 1852, a late spring snow blocked all trails, nearly starving the trapped miners. Floods and fire forced the town's relocation to the bluff overlooking the Salmon's junction with the Klamath. Today at Somes Bar there is another of those wonderful general stores, offering the locals and traveler alike a great array of sundries.

For ancient Karuk Indians, this awesome spot at the confluence of the Salmon and Klamath rivers was the Center of the Universe. In their language *karuk* means "upriver" *yuruk* "downriver", *maruk* "uphill away from the river", and *saruk* "toward the river". The bountiful harvest from waters of these rivers was such an important part of their lives that their calendar year began with the fall run, when they caught the fish in nets strung between stout poles.

From the bridge spanning the two rivers, you can see Ishi Pishi Falls leap-frogging over a mass of water-worn boulders. This quarter-mile stretch of rocks and rapids is the reason the Klamath can't be completely navigated by river runners without a portage. Below the confluence, the seven miles of the river to Orleans offers a Grand Canyon-type experience. The gorge opens up dramatically and rafters can thrill to the adventures of Class 3 (requires complex maneuvering) and Class 2 (requires a few basic boating skills) rapids before settling into the more sedate waters above Orleans.

The Salmon River, however, is something else again! According to an excellent guide, *Life on the River*, published by Orleans Chamber of Commerce, the "Slammin' Salmon" offers some of the most difficult and exciting whitewater in the state for experienced rafters in good condition. The river features both Class 5 (runnable for experts only) and Class 4 (technically arduous but not as life threatening) rapids, aptly named Freight Train, Last Chance, Achilles Heel, and Whirling Dervish.

An intriguing sign on a road leading off to the east beckons to Oak Bottom Campground 2 miles—Forks of the Salmon 17 miles. Although accessible by car or RV, the oak-shaded campground is on a hillside above and across from the river and is heavily used by rafters during summer season. The rest of the road heading east is exceedingly narrow and winding. (I haven't ventured on it but a friend described the trip as one of those "ohmigawd, how did I get here and how do I get out?" experiences.) From the Forks of the Salmon, two roads wind their crooked ways between the Marble Mountain Wilderness

NUT HATCH

LADY SLIPPER

and the Trinity Alps Wilderness, exiting on Highway 3. I do not recommend these routes, even if they appear on the AAA and California state maps to be reasonable ways to traverse the Klamath Mountains.

For 40 miles after leaving Somes Bar, Highway 96 plays tag with the river as it jogs its contorted way northward toward Happy Camp. Less than halfway Dillon Creek Campground provides a respite. In the campground a narrow, gravel road shaded by large oaks and madrones meanders along the creekbank. On my walks, I look for those special plants endemic to this area and have spotted the magenta blossoms of currant bushes and the pouch-shaped white bloom of the mountain lady slipper. I have watched a nuthatch pick its dainty way head first down a tree trunk and have startled a family of quail from its hiding place. As I said hi to a family of campers, grilling fresh-caught trout, they told me "it's a good fishin' creek." (No, they didn't invite me to join them.) Locals know this campground for its large swimming hole boasting crystal clear water and a high cliff of rocks to dive from.

As you proceed, watch for signs designating other walking areas. Several lead to waterfalls. For a short side jaunt, a bridge on the right will take you across the river to Independence, a once profitable mine with a bunkhouse for its twenty-some workers. Just beyond is Ferry Point, where a small community flourished in the mid-1850s with a hotel, store, school, and a ferry that shuttled freight wagons and mule packers across the river. They used to come all the way from the coast and the South Fork of the Smith River along the Kelsey Trail, lurching over the Siskiyous to the settlements on the other side of the Marble Mountains. An incredible journey!

There are other river access points along this route, and I have stopped often to watch in admiration as rafters swirl in the currents of the rapids: Dragons Teeth, Sasquatch Squeeze, Exterminator, Devil's Toenail, and Rattlesnake. I have no desire to be tossed about in those little rubber boats, but I do rather envy the rafters' youth and exuberance. These specks of humanity, challenging the power of the river, affirm the continuation and vitality of life.

As one nears Happy Camp, it is always a pleasure to drive beside the calmer, more benign waters of the upper Klamath River.

STATE OF JEFFERSON SCENIC BYWAY

Chapter V
STATE OF JEFFERSON SCENIC BYWAY
California State Highway 96
108 Miles

The two names originally given to the town at the terminus of the Bigfoot Scenic Byway (locals claim it is the *bookend gateway*, with Willow Creek at its other end) reflect its checkered past. Settled in 1851, the name Happy Camp emerged from the elation of prospectors finding gold in the creeks, and the name Murderer's Bar arose from fatal disputes between claim jumpers. Although the Happy name stuck, the camp's big dreams popped like colorful balloons. As with other settlements around the Northern Diggings, when gold strikes dwindled, miners moved out.

However, its important location on the Klamath River gave the town a second chance, the chance to be the hub of the State of Jefferson. In the early 1940s, three of California's northernmost counties, and one in Oregon, rebelled against their respective state governments, claiming lack of assistance in developing passable roads into their isolated areas. This issue of secession was not new. The State of Jefferson was preceded by an effort to form the State of Shasta in 1852, and the State of Klamath in 1853.

Their grudge was not without merit. When the botanist-geologist William Brewer attempted to survey a route along the Klamath in 1863, he wrote: *No wagon road enters these parts, only a rough trail, dusty with deep ruts in summer, wet and muddy in winter.* After several more feeble attempts to secede in the early 1900s, the final threat came in November 1941. To bring public attention to their plight, the rebels placed barricades across the troublesome route leading west from Yreka. The bombing of Pearl Harbor put an end to that dream, but the symbol of double crosses, XX, to express the feeling of being double-crossed by the two states, remains today.

Happy Camp's third chance for prosperity depended upon the timber industry, loggers replacing miners and sawmills replacing dredgers. Unfortunately, when regulations against timber harvesting closed the sawmills, business establishments suffered and many residents moved away. But somehow, Happy Camp survived. Again, its significant location midway on a scenic byway, designated in 1992, has given the town a fourth opportunity to flourish. But, for the kind of tourists who need luxurious accommodations or commercial entertainment to enjoy their vacation, this is not the place for them. For an outdoor enthusiast, this *is* the place: a prime area for fishing and boating, camping and horse-packing, birding and botanizing, hiking and biking, rock hounding, and gold panning. And, especially for folks who love to explore back roads that wander helter-skelter through untamed lands, all of this border country will more than meet their expectations.

Long before gold miners, timber harvesters, governmental malcontents, or recreationists invaded this remote area, the entire territory was ancestral homeland of the Karuk Tribe. As you learned on your journey up the Klamath, native villages spread along the river from its confluence with the Trinity, north to Happy Camp and beyond.

Since finally receiving federal recognition 25 years ago, the Karuks have become a valuable asset to the community. Through an abundance of grants involving substantial sums of money to the Karuk Community Development Corporation, the tribe has embarked on an extensive building program. Facilities have been provided for housing and health services, a Head Start program for children and a nutrition program for Elders, a cultural, interpretive center to display traditional artifacts, and the Happy Camp Community Computer Center.

I suggest a visit to the new tribal administration building on the left side of Highway 96, just before entering Happy Camp. Its long, low construction, reminiscent of ancient Indian structures, would certainly meet the approval of Frank Lloyd Wright, the architect who so successfully united his buildings with the land. A receptionist in the main office can give you more information about tribal enterprises and will perhaps suggest traditional ceremonies you might attend.

Happy Camp

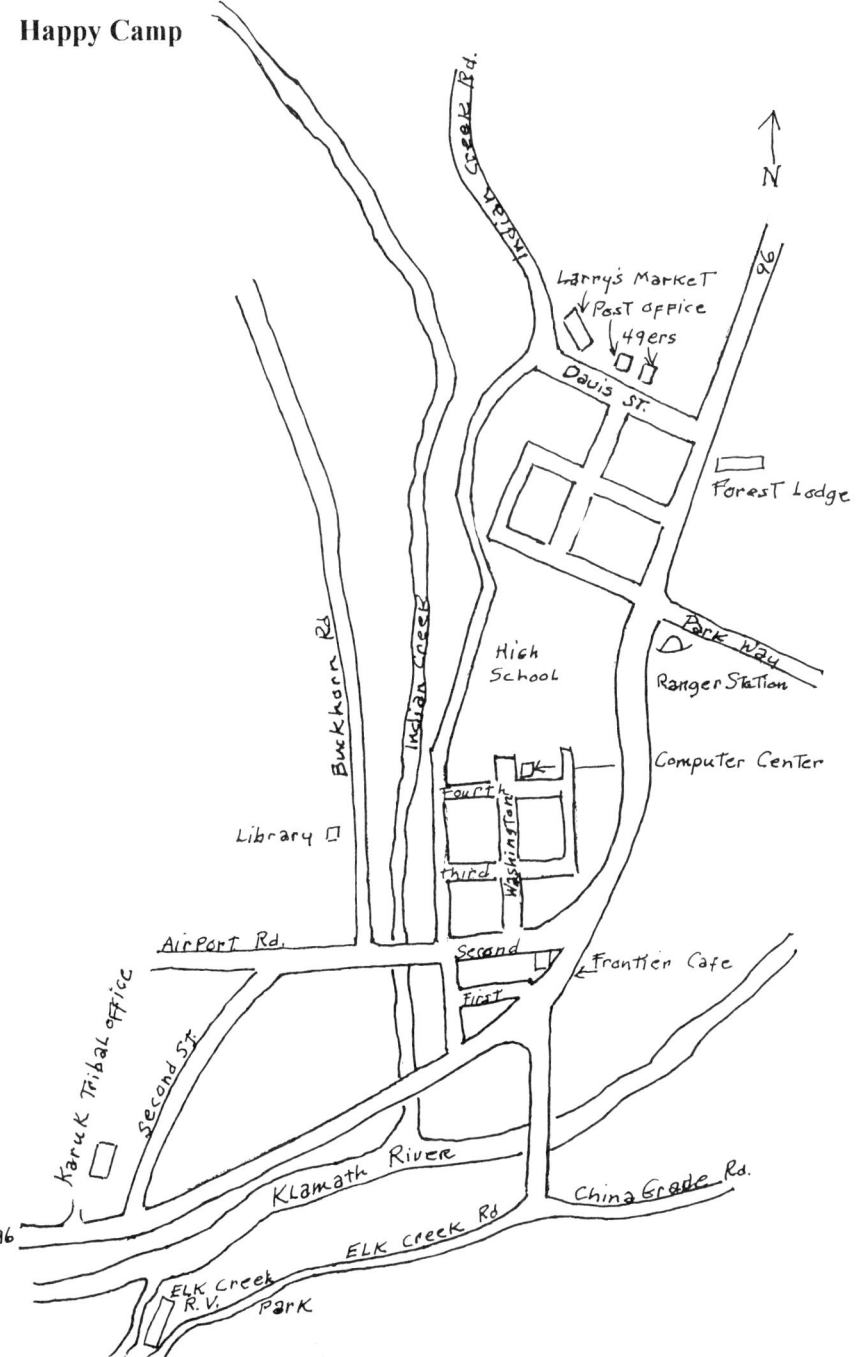

When I first discovered Happy Camp, I wondered if a region or a town could be said to have character. The *Oxford Dictionary* defines the word as "the collective qualities, mental and moral, that distinguish a person or a thing," with no mention of place. So what defines the Western writer Wallace Stegner's sense of place? The definition would be subjective, a personal response to a mountain, a river, or a town. Do they manifest an esoteric spirit, a special energy? Does Happy Camp? Yes. This village exemplifies a remarkable character: independence and individuality. It is unpretentious but not without culture, unforgettable but not distinguished. In fact, it's a bit funky, a bit quirky. *Ya gotta love it!*

To understand my feeling, cruise the roads that wander off Highway 96. You might become confused but you won't get lost—at least, not for long. As you approach the town from the south, turn left on Second Avenue, and left again on Airport Road to take a quick look at the Happy Camp Airport. Located on what was known as Schoolhouse Flat in 1880, it offers a mini-runway for private planes and provides space for an active heliport, used by the forest service for spotting and controlling ever-threatening fires. The Mercy Flight helicopter for flying out the injured and sick also uses the airport, if a closer landing spot is not possible.

Following Airport Road back toward town, turn left on Indian Creek Road and walk the short blocks of the historic district—First, Second, and Third Avenues. Visit Evans Mercantile, a family-owned business since 1959, a little bit of everything place: clothes and shoes, greeting cards, postcards and gifts, and lots of free chit-chat about the town's history. You will be advised to observe the mural on the parking-lot side of the building, one of several painted by Diann Hokanson. (You will see others as you drive through the town.)

On the corner of Second Avenue be sure to notice an old brick structure, built well over a century ago by James Camp and John Titus as the supply center for townsfolk. On the opposite corner, a dilapidated, gabled, clapboard building with tacked-on, shedlike additions was once a stagecoach inn. The sad remains of the old Cuddihy Hotel should be awarded an historic preservation grant to restore it to its former status.

THE AMERICA HOUSE / CUDDIHY HOTEL

When I prowled around Happy Camp in search of the county library, I crossed the bridge over Indian Creek and turned right on Buckhorn Road. Unfortunately, the tiny library was closed on that day. Instead I parked across from the town cemetery, its chain-link fence covered with brilliantly blooming roses. A walkabout revealed the carefully tended gravesites of pioneer families, their names now identifying several town streets.

Back on Indian Creek Road, I turned north again to pass the high school and the aforementioned Computer Center. To visit the latter, I turned off Indian Creek Road on to Fourth Avenue and followed it to Washington, where I found the building on the corner. The attendant on duty explained the free program for the public and kindly printed several pages of information about the classes offered.

After returning to Indian Creek and following it a short ways, a right turn put me on Davis Road, apparently serving as the town's Main Street—other than Highway 96. Here (if you are following my circumnavigation of the town) you will find the well-stocked Larry's Market and a 100 foot-long mural by Diann Hokanson depicting the history of Happy Camp on the outside wall. In the same parking area is the post office, guarded by a statue of Bigfoot, and next to it, The New 49'ers Prospecting Organization. (If you are interested in gold mining, this is the place to go for basic training workshops. See appendix for contact information.) Next door the Siskiyou House, a mini museum selling antiques, gifts, and collectibles, provides visitor information.

At the end of Davis Road, turn south again onto the highway to find the local bank, a couple of stores, and another mural, an exciting portrayal of white-water riverrunners. And that's what is so wonderful about this little town. No matter where you are, you can soon hear the sound of rippling water, sniff air pungent with the scent of evergreens, or gaze upon the lush mountains. For information about campgrounds and maps for hiking trails into the Marble Mountains, surrounded by the Klamath National Forest, drop into the Happy Camp District Ranger's Office on the corner of Park Way.

The Marbles have been described as *old and wizened, their rocks folded, faulted and upthrust.* Composed of granite, slate, and chert once deposited on the ocean floor, their crags are sharp and canyons V-shaped. Cascading streams plummet down these steep-walled gorges into narrow valleys, humpy with boulders and sparsely decorated with green meadows.

Perhaps the easiest way to experience such grandeur is to go south again on Highway 96, turn left on Elk Creek Road and cross the river, turning right to follow the road up into the hills. After a mile, I suggest a visit to the miniature horse farm at Little Dreams Ranch, owned and operated by Jean and Eddie Davenport. As an adjunct to Elk Creek Campground (my home when I'm in the area), it is pure delight to watch these tiny, perfect animals romp around their pasture or trot smartly along campground roads, towing little carts.

Eddie informed me that Elk Creek is aptly named. After elks were nearly decimated by expanding population and over-hunting, these stately animals have been re-introduced to the area and are apparently coming south again from Oregon. During the Davenports' first winter in residence, they spotted a herd moving slowly down to water under a bridge, five miles upriver. One of the summer hikes they recommend is to drive up Elk Creek Road 10 miles to another bridge, cross it and stay right until you come to a parking area. They don't promise you'll catch sight of a herd, but do suggest you follow the jeep tracks about a quarter mile to the end and walk down the path to a beautiful waterfall.

The Jefferson State Scenic Byway doesn't start or end at Happy Camp but veers northwest for 38 miles to dead-end at Highway 199. This is a splendid drive, traversing the Siskiyou Mountains that run along the Oregon border, and turn south, separating the Klamath and Smith rivers. The route not only runs between the Red Butte Wilderness and the Siskiyou Wilderness (both protected, roadless areas) but also transports you through a wealth of biologically diverse plant and wildlife zones.

Leaving town on Indian Creek Road (also called Grayback Road, closed in winter), it's an easy but slow trip all the way, following the creek for 11 miles before beginning to climb. The first time I ventured up Grayback, there was a gaping maw on the downhill side of the road, and I cautiously inched around the bend. The next time, the hole had been filled in, repaired, and repaved to a smooth, more graceful curve.

Numerous forest service roads leading off this route provide access to small lakes, old mines, abandoned hamlets, botanical research areas, and campgrounds with a maze of nature trails. Watch for thick clumps of dogwood blooming along banks and, as you gain elevation, groups of sugar pine, with their long cones hanging from the ends of branches, and Douglas fir, with small, hairy-looking cones, supported by flat-needled branches. You should be able to distinguish between the white fir with its short, curving needles and cones standing up along the branches and the red fir, commonly called the silver tip or Christmas tree. Traveling higher, watch for the stunted, thick-trunk foxtail pine and bushes of heather (evocative of Scotland). Be sure to stop at the scenic turnout to look for the rare weeping or Brewer's spruce (loveliest of all conifers, in my opinion), its slender feathery branches and long cones stretching for the ground.

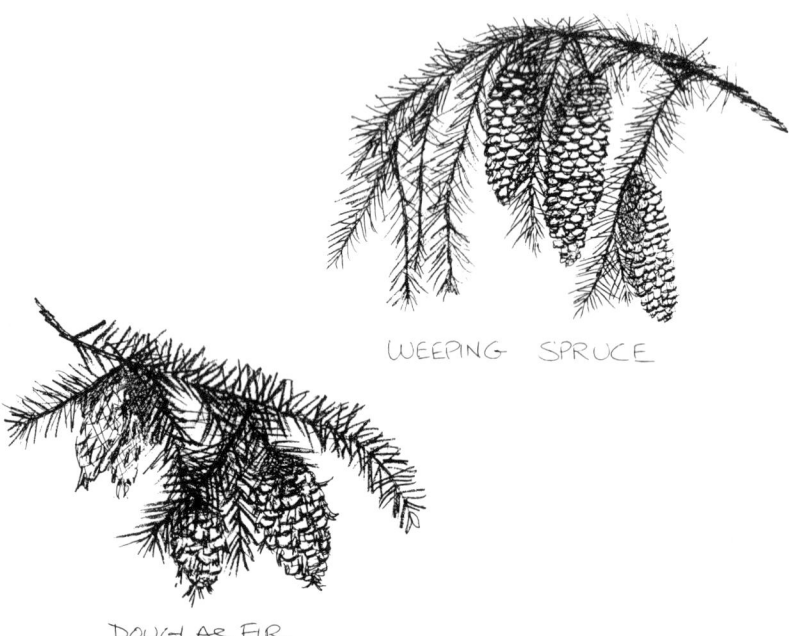

WEEPING SPRUCE

DOUGLAS FIR

After driving 22 miles from Happy Camp, you will reach the summit (elev. 4812 ft.), affording glimpses of the snowcapped Marble Mountains to the east. It's an easy 16-mile drift down into Oregon and the end (or beginning) of the State of Jefferson Scenic Byway. Where it meets Highway 199, you can turn left for the short drive along the Smith River Scenic Byway to reach Highway 101 or you can backtrack.

If you return to Happy Camp, three miles before reaching town you may notice a discreet sign on the right advertising Indian Creek Trailer Park. As you turn in and bear right, you'll see a plain pale mustard, sprawling building, home of *Naturegraph: Books for a Better World.* Barbara Brown, owner, publisher, and widow of founder Vinson Brown, kindly invites visitors to tour this incredible establishment. The 10,000 square-foot structure houses a series of rooms, one opening into another. Shelves are stocked with bundles of books ready for distributing and tables are laden with stacks of paper, ready for running through the large printing press. There are machines for folding, cutting, and binding, and a darkroom containing photographic equipment. After printing, the beautifully designed covers are sent out to be laminated.

As a reflection of Vinson Brown's training in Natural History and his intense interest in Native Americans, Naturegraph's catalog features numerous books on Native Americans and on wildlife and birds, rocks and minerals, and even recipe books for edible wild plants.

As you leave town heading east on Highway 96, note the Welcome to Happy Camp sign on the left, where the old route wanders off under the oaks toward town. The highway then curves around bends in the river, with a pastoral view to vivid green meadows on the other bank. A couple of side roads lead down to the Klamath, put-in points for boaters: Gordon's Ferry Road (not a through road, one mile) and China Point, high above the river (RVs not advised).

Ten miles from Happy Camp, Thompson Creek flows into the river. At this confluence today, it's hard to imagine a three-mile aerial tramway bringing loads of copper ore down from Gray Eagle Mine, to be hauled eastward over those unpassable roads during the 1940s. It's also hard to imagine a troop of soldiers marching through these rugged canyons, en route to the Rogue Valley Indian

Wars in 1860. However, evidence remains in a fence-enclosed cemetery resting quietly on the hillside above Fort Goff, site of the temporary military camp, now a forest service walk-in campground.

Just beyond, at Portuguese Creek, you may notice the absence of vegetation, the result of the floodwaters of 1997. Trees were torn from hillsides and huge boulders calved like glaciers, piling rocky barriers across the highway, cutting off the supply route for all communities between Horse Creek and Orleans—a distance of 83 miles.

Just before entering Seiad you will note on the right a large white building marked *The Wildwood*. Built as a tavern in 1924, it acquired a dubious reputation during the ensuing years and the building was sadly neglected. Completely renovated in 2000, with the addition of a "to code" kitchen, it is now a delightful place to dine. Owner-chef Rita Herbst serves a host of loyal customers who drive for miles to sample her delicious creations. Her sister, Carol Williams, brought me a bowl of the best French onion soup I have ever tasted and told me about a third sister, also a fabulous cook, located farther east along the river.

Having wended its way southward from the Oregon border along the crest of the Siskiyous, the Pacific Crest Trail emerges just across from the Wildwood under a grove of live oaks. It follows the highway the short distance to Seiad Valley, a pick-up location for PCT hikers. You can just bet the place bustles with activity as hikers pick up their mail and stock up on fresh supplies. The Pacific Crest Trail continues along the highway, crosses over the Klamath River and at Grider Creek turns right and continues southward. The trail then snakes its way 40 miles through the Marble Mountains, one of the first designated wilderness areas in the state. It crosses both forks of the Salmon River, with the Russian Wilderness in between. This rare bit of protected country encloses the largest concentration of conifers in the world, 17 species, and more than a dozen pristine lakes. You will encounter The Pacific Crest Trail again on the Trinity Heritage Byway at Scott Mountain Summit.

Seiad Valley is as pretty a scene as is to be found anywhere along the river. Once the site of the easternmost Karuk village, it embodies the Indian meaning of the name, peaceful valley. During his travels in 1863, Surveyor William Brewer admitted he was well fed by local

farmers, but wrote: *There is nothing here to make the region ever a desirable home for any considerable population.* He should see it now. I explored the back road up Seiad Creek, stopping to take a photo of a flock of geese strutting and preening in a meadow and another of a well-preserved old barn. I passed dairy cows and beef cattle and orchards ripe with apples, pears, and plums, before returning to the highway and paying my respects to the town.

Admittedly, the town is small (population 350) but it does include a cardlock gas pump across the road from a two-story, dingy-white building with a rusted metal roof and a sign, Old Seiad Store. Just beyond is the new Seiad Valley Store & Restaurant, Official Pacific Crest Trail Midway Point.

Two miles past Seiad, the river pulls away from Highway 96 to leave a loop of farmland watered by Grider Creek, named for an early homesteader. I turned off the highway to follow Grider Creek Road, on the lookout for the Pacific Crest Trail coming down the mountain and, hopefully, any one of the aquatic birds known to nest among the alders. As I pulled up beside the river, a harsh *kraaank* melded with the soft ripply sounds of water and a great blue heron snatched a fish in its scissorlike bill, rose slowly, stretched its long thin legs behind its body, and lazily flapped away downstream.

After Grider Creek Road, the highway follows the river on the south side for seven miles to Hamburg, named by a homesick German miner. Today, with one store and a population of 80, it's hard to imagine 5000 persons filling the village in the 1880s or to believe that Zane Gray tossed down a drink in the Bucket of Blood Saloon during the 1930s.

East of Hamburg, at the junction of Highway 96 and the Scott River Road, you will note a gathering place for campers, motor homes, trailers, and tents, all providing temporary housing for members of gold prospecting clubs. I recommend a three-mile side jaunt up the Scott River road where you might be able to watch modern miners in action. After you pass a 1915 wood-plank bridge crossing Scott River and drive a mile or so south, you can park beside Scott Bar's Community Center, located in a white-with-blue-trim old schoolhouse.

HORSE CREEK SUSPENSION BRIDGE

A short walk uphill will take you past a display of rusted mining equipment and what must be the state's smallest post office. Across the road is a bronze plaque set into a large boulder and enclosed by a wrought-iron fence. The marker extols John Scott's rich gold strike, the largest nugget ever found in the river that bears his name: 187 ounces, worth over $18 per ounce.

After returning to Highway 96 and driving five miles, be on the lookout for Horse Creek. Legend says the creek got its name because a mountain lion attacked and killed a horse belonging to a Shasta Indian, but perhaps it should be called Four Bridges. When the place was settled, a cable-suspension footbridge was built to provide access to gulches across the river. The first bridge was replaced in 1901 by a wooden bridge and, when it fell into the water, another suspension bridge was built. A mile farther, a modern highway bridge crosses the Klamath, with a wide turnout providing parking for oak-shaded picnic tables and Brown Bear River Access Point.

For the next eight miles, the road closely follows the river on the north side and conifers gradually become sparse and oak woodland and chaparral dot the hillsides. In this drier environment the sudden appearance of vivid green lawns across the river is startling. The nine-hole Eagles Nest Golf Course can be reached by crossing a bridge to Walker Road and following it east for half a mile.

After the Walker Road bridge, the area of Klamath River borders both banks of the river for 11 miles. Watch for the Sportsman's Lodge on the right, the restaurant now operated by new owners, the third sister chef and her husband, Kay and David Hodges. Kay has been catering for more than 30 years and prepares family-style meals to rave reviews.

This community was once an important trade center for miners and a source of bootleg whiskey, stored in abandoned gold-mine tunnels. The Quigley General Store, built by one of the moonshiners in the 1920s, is still doing a brisk business, supplying sundries for residents of the several trailer parks lining the riverbanks. Whiskey too? I didn't ask but did enjoy a cup of coffee with a slice of fresh blackberry pie. The store's pies and cakes, served at the deli, are freshly home-baked and delicious.

Ten miles beyond, and down a short, steep road on the south side of Highway 96, is the Tree of Heaven forest

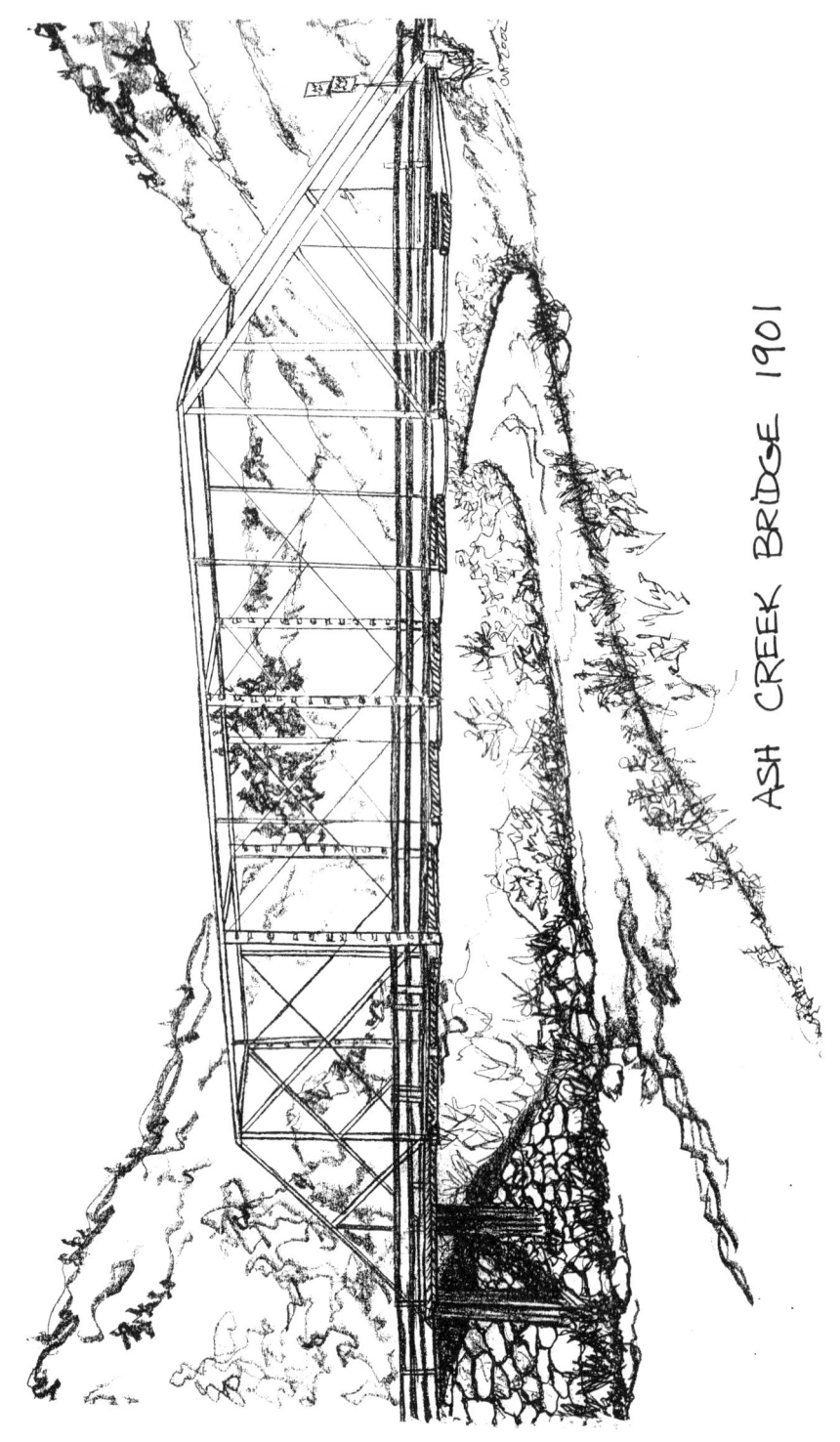

ASH CREEK BRIDGE 1901

service campground, named for the feathery-leafed tree imported by the Chinese who farmed the flatland along the river. One of the few public "hosted" campgrounds, supervised by a couple who drive north every summer from Arizona, you know that it is special. The 22 camping sites are surrounded by well-tended lawns and shaded by a wonderful variety of trees: oak and broad leaf maple, pine and cedar, locust, sycamore, and a Sequoia redwood. The campground also provides a playground and picnic area for day-trippers and a ramp for launching canoes and kayaks.

One of the special aspects of this park is the wheelchair-friendly interpretive trail winding through the willows and alders along the riverbank. Beautifully designed signs provide information about the neotropical migratory birds that follow the Klamath as their Western flyway: geese and mergansers, hummingbirds, flycatchers, and warblers. Resident bird species are the osprey, blue heron, red-tailed hawk, and belted kingfisher.

Beaver are common residents along the Klamath, but the only evidence I saw were several dams, humps of stick and mud forming little ponds, and the gnawed cone-shaped tree stumps left behind. While sitting beside the river one evening, I did enjoy watching a pair of otters and what fun they seemed to be having, frolicking in a game of tag.

The State of Jefferson Scenic Byway ends three miles east of the campground, at the confluence of the Shasta River with the Klamath. You are only two miles from the on-ramp to I-5, but I suggest you turn right on Highway 263 and pull into an overlook for a view of the original stagecoach trail far below and the old Ash Creek Bridge, built in 1901. For an admirer of feisty people and a devotee of old, single-lane bridges such as I, this scenic byway is always a satisfying journey.

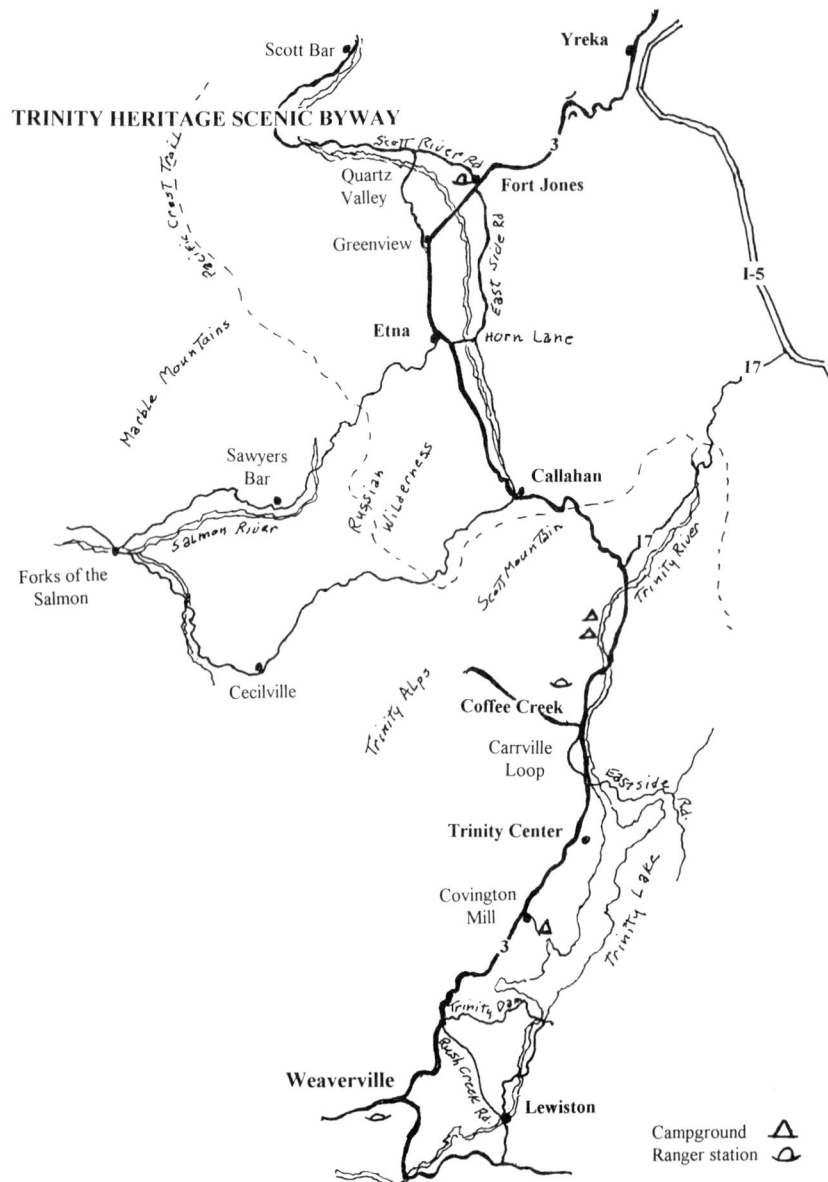

Chapter VI
TRINITY HERITAGE SCENIC BYWAY
California State Highway 3
120 Miles

As you cross the Pioneer Bridge and head south on Highway 263, marvel at this 1930s masterpiece of engineering, blasted from craggy rock walls through a tortuous gorge. The view across the river of barren lava-pocked hillsides, barely covered with stunted sage brush, is far different from the thick, green forests you have been traveling through. After you have navigated your way up the canyon and over three more bridges, make a right turn for a quick look at Hawkinsville. This mining camp, once called Frogtown (for reasons unknown to me), rates a stop, if only to photograph a charming redbrick Catholic church, sanctified in 1877 from an old store built in 1858.

This portion of the Trinity Heritage Scenic Byway does not actually begin at Yreka, but if you have had enough wild and scenic vistas, this larger town, providing more amenities, will be a pleasant contrast. If you were zipping south on I-5, you might have been tempted to pass it by, but it is definitely worth a stopover. Highway 263 becomes Yreka's Main Street. Once you arrive, I suggest a visit to the Tourist Information Center on the corner of Miner and Broadway, one block west of Main. There you can learn everything you might want to know about Yreka and Siskiyou County, California's third largest county in land size.

No attempt will be made in this chapter to relate Yreka's history, as rich in gold dust lore as any in the Northern Diggings. The vast array of flyers and brochures available to a visitor include a detailed account of the city's beginnings and a walking-tour guide of the historic district. After perusing all the literature gathered, you can decide what interests you most for a walkabout: the residential streets with more than 75 homes listed on the National Register of Historic Places; the midtown commercial district with its redbrick, balconied buildings; the display of gold nuggets in the county courthouse on the corner of Butte and Oregon streets; or a replica of a traditional Indian sweat lodge in the Native American Heritage Park on North Miner, adjacent to the fire department.

Because I'm a history buff, my exploration of Yreka began in the Siskiyou County Museum. Built to resemble the 1854 Callahan Ranch Hotel, this well-organized museum includes two separate galleries, a conference room, research library, and gift shop. (Hint: buy a postcard picture of the museum to compare with the original Callahan Hotel, which you will see as you drive south on Highway 3.)

The Native American Gallery features the cultural histories and artistry of local tribes: Karuk, Shasta, and Modoc. The Trappers' Gallery exhibits items used by the men who came into the north country in search of fur-bearing animals. An outdoor museum displays nineteenth-century buildings relocated from various parts of Siskiyou County: a blacksmith shop, a schoolhouse, and a miner's cabin, among others. The Yreka Creek Greenway runs behind the museum, a delightful trail for leg-stretching, picnicking, or simply bench-sitting.

A drive south on Main Street and a left turn on East Oberlin Street (under the I-5 overpass) to the corner of Fairlane took me to the Klamath National Forest Headquarters—and a major disappointment. Their much touted interpretive museum containing "one of the most extensive collections of natural and historical exhibits in any National Forest in the United States" was no longer open to visitors. Again, major cutbacks in federal funding. Perhaps you might visit during a more affluent time, but you can, at least, gather more information about camping, fishing, hiking, and hunting in the Klamath Mountains.

Driving back to Main Street and continuing south to Greenhorn Road led me to Greenhorn Reservoir Park, a wildlife haven and angler's delight. There is a parking area large enough for RVs, a playground for children, picnic tables, and a map detailing a walk along an old mining strip, with reconstructed cabins similar to those lining Miner Street in the boom days.

For a "let someone else do the driving" excursion, nothing could be more delightful than a *toot-toot* 15-mile, three-hour round-trip ride to Montague on the *Blue Goose*, a train pulled by a steam locomotive. In continuous operation since 1889, the short-line track was Yreka's answer to being bypassed by Southern Pacific Company's route from Oregon into California. While waiting for the "all aboard," you can visit the renovated depot train museum.

As you leave Yreka southward, Main Street becomes Fort Jones Road and Highway 3, traversing a three-mile-long valley, where cone-shaped conifers stud the hills above a dust ruffle of oaks fringing the meadows and pastures below. The highway gradually climbs to Forest Summit and a vista-point turnout. Take out your Northern California map to get an inkling of the grandeur that surrounds you. In the distance to the north are the Siskiyous, once a formidable barrier between California and Oregon. In the west, the magnificent Marble Mountains (or as a brochure described them, *glacier-gouged goliaths*) tower over the valley floor. Away to the southwest loom the Salmon Mountains, cut at their base by two forks of the Salmon River, and directly south, the Scott Mountains, forming the northern edge of the Trinity Alps.

This awesome area was originally inhabited by the Shasta Indians, sharing its bounties with the Karuks, both tribes of the Hokan linguistic group. In the mid-1830s, white men invaded their lands, following their trails in search of beaver. These included Hudson's Bay fur trapper Peter Skene Ogden, who scoured the rivers for valuable pelts for rich men's hats, and Ewing Young, who drove a herd of 700 cattle from San Francisco to the Willamette Valley to fill rich men's bellies.

Directly below Forest Summit lies Scott Valley, the jewel in the crown of Northern California. This fertile meadowland was once a lake, the result of beavers diligently building dams, and so it was aptly named Beaver Valley by the trappers. It was rediscovered in the 1850s and given its new name by John Scott's group of prospectors, working their way up the Scott River from its junction with the Klamath. At the north end of the valley is Fort Jones, a garrison established in 1852 to protect the trappers, miners, and settlers from avenging Indian raids.

Scott Valley was also the domain of other notable men. Stephen Hall Meek, guide for emigrant wagon trains, trapped, hunted, and died in the valley in 1889 at age 82. Joaquin Miller, a gold miner on the Klamath and Scott rivers, became famous as *The Poet of the Sierras*. Quartermaster George Crook served duty-time at Fort Jones in 1853. He achieved the rank of Major General during the Civil War and fame for the capture of Apache war leader, Geronimo.

Be sure to visit the Fort Jones Museum in the middle of town on the west side of Main Street. (A sketch of bushy-bearded Stephen Hall Meek, and a copy of his signature, grace the cover of the museum's flyer.) Inside the small building you will see a fine collection of artifacts depicting the lives of the Shasta Indians, miners, trappers, and early settlers. The construction of the outside rock walls is really special and reads like a history of the entire region: mortars, pestles, and gristmill stones plowed up in Quartz Valley; petrified wood, minerals, and remnants of a meteorite; copper ore, slabs of iron-pyrite and black obsidian, jade and marble; and fossilized fish, snails, mollusks, and eels.

FORT JONES

Although only a monument designates the site of the original fort, today the town is clean and sprightly, its baker's dozen historic buildings spread along five or six blocks of Main Street. As you enter town from the north, turn left up Sterling Street to East Street, park in front of the Community Center, and visit the Methodist Church built in 1875, and the Carriage House, displaying seven horse-drawn vehicles. The Fort Jones Branch of the

Siskiyou County Library is located near the end of East Street.

Dominating Main Street is the 128-foot wooden flagpole next to the Willard Building, a 1920s general store. On the corner of Main and Newton, the two-story brick structure, built in 1860 by A. B. Carlock, served as a dry goods store, with the Masonic Lodge above. Across the street is the Scott Valley Bank, the second oldest banking institution in California, and across Horn Street is the 1850 Fort Jones House, a stage stop on the Oregon-California Trail.

Because I feel that driving through and around Scott Valley (28 miles long and 6 miles wide) is such an interesting experience, I'm suggesting several side trips. You will see incredibly green pastures sheltered by groves of ancient oaks; elegant Victorian homes and sprawling ranch houses, many still owned by descendants of the settlers; split-rail fences enclosing barns, sheds and old farm wagons, and fields of golden grain, harvested and rolled into rounds. And you may unexpectedly spot ostriches, llamas, alpacas, and buffalo in addition to Herefords and Black Angus cattle.

A long, but scenic side trip is the Scott River Road which follows the Scott River to its junction with the Klamath. As you head northwest out of Fort Jones, stop at the ranger station on the left side of Scott River Road to gather information about trails into the Marble Mountains and other recreational opportunities in the Scott River District of the Klamath National Forest. You can follow the paved but narrow and twisty road, riding high above the river as it cuts through an awesome gorge for 31 miles to Highway 96. No doubt locals hot-rod the route with impunity, but I traveled it only once on a late afternoon, after a long day of driving. As lengthening shadows cut across the crumbling edges of storm-damaged asphalt, I begged my over worked guardian angels to once more keep me safe.

A shorter and safer side trip will take you around the equally scenic Quartz Valley loop, beginning at its junction with the Scott River Road, seven miles from Highway 3. (Note the old Meamber Schoolhouse on the corner.) At the time Fort Jones was built, a treaty was signed between the military and the Shasta Indians—a treaty never ratified by the government. Under the Indian Reorganization Act of 1937, a tribal reservation was established in Quartz Valley—a reservation that was terminated in 1960. As the land was individually deeded to members of the tribe, many promptly sold their property. Twenty years later, the termination was declared unlawful and the reservation was legally reinstated. A sign on a gated road leading back into the woods midway on the loop reads, "U.S. Trust Property. Department of the Interior. Bureau of Indian Affairs. No admittance."

The valley was appropriately named for the valuable quartz mined in the 1860s, with Mugginsville as its hub, supporting a gristmill, store, hotel, and blacksmith shop. Passing by the almost nonexistent town today, it's hard to visualize it as the site of eight stamp mills busily crushing gold-bearing ore. This 10-mile loop you've been traveling ends at Greenview, originally named Hayes Corner for the family who homesteaded the land. (I wonder why so many of the old names didn't survive?)

At this junction with Highway 3, I suggest you go back five miles toward Fort Jones, turn right on Eastside Road, pass the site of the old fort, and make a left turn up to the cemetery. A stroll among the tombstones is like turning the pages of a history book, revealing insights into prominent families. After returning to Eastside Road, continue south, gently winding around the base of the foothills for 12 miles to Horn Lane. Cross the river and turn north to visit Etna, tucked into a spectacular basin at the foot of Whiskey Butte and Etna Mountain.

As the terminus of the tortuous pack-train trail tracking the North Fork of the Salmon River, 40 miles from Forks of the Salmon and 57 miles from Somes Bar, Etna sprang to life as a supply center for miners streaming over the summit. Its earlier name, Rough and Ready, certainly seemed appropriate, and its rich pastoral farmland, flour mill, and Kappler Brewery assured its prosperity—until the brewery's closure during prohibition. Today a modern micro-brewery, Etna Brewing Co. uses the same label as the original and is located on the same spot.

Etna's atmosphere is very 1930s, reminiscent of everyone's ideal hometown. A newspaper columnist described it as *a real-life country village, where blue bachelor buttons grow like weeds and swallows nest under the eaves of the old buildings.* Many of these old buildings remain and I suggest you begin a walking tour at the tall flagpole beside the museum on Main Street. Moving down Main, you will pass the Masonic Hall, built in 1867 (at the cost of $3000) and the Knights of Pythias Hall, built in 1929 on the site of the Rough and Ready flour mill. Cross the street and walk back up Main, passing a whole block of brick, stone, and wood structures built in 1877.

At the corner of Main and Diggles, drop into the Scott Valley Drug Store, and treat yourself to ice cream at the marble counter of a soda fountain that came across the prairie by schooner wagon in 1876. The store is full of all sorts of take-home-to-friends-and-family items, as well as answers to any questions you might ask about the town's history. As you proceed up Main Street, you will pass a number of lovely Victorian homes, including an elegant bed-and-breakfast inn, Bradley's Alderbrook Manor. Built in the late 1800s by Elza Eller, who carried mail and freight over the Salmon Mountains, it has been impeccably maintained by only two other occupants.

Etna has a rather confusing group of streets going every which way, appearing on its "Historic Homes Walk Tour Map" like a modern architectural structure with add-ons. However, the town is easily drivable. To view several more Victorian houses, simply wander at your will. Especially notable is the Balfrey home at 384 Center Street, built by a pharmacist for his bride-to-be, first woman graduate of Stanford University and Siskiyou County's first Superintendent of Schools. (It was also the first house in Etna with an indoor water closet.)

Before you leave Etna, you could, if you're fearless or foolhardy, (and not driving a huge motor home or hauling a trailer) explore the Salmon River Road southwest out of town. The views of the Marbles, the Trinities, and the Russian Wilderness are spectacular along this route—so I've been told. The upper portion is 29 miles via steep grades over a 6,000-foot summit to Sawyer's Bar, heart of the Northern Mines. Still standing is a tall, peaked-roof, wooden Catholic Church, with steep steps leading up and into the sanctuary. According to local legend, it was built in 1855 atop an estimated $200,000 in placer gold. Another 12 miles of curvy driving will take you to Forks of the Salmon and the junction of a 48-mile road returning eastward to Highway 3 via Cecilville to Callahan.

Driving Highway 3 south from Etna to Callahan, gaining only 200 feet in elevation in 13 miles, may not be as

wildly scenic, but it is a safer route. Another choice is to retrace Horn Lane out of Etna to Callahan Road on the east side of the river and follow the old Oregon to California Trail, in use from 1852 to 1871. Fenced pastures and lovely old homes, including a stagecoach stopover, the Ohio Stage Station, add to the charm of this farm-to-market road.

At the upper end of Scott River, you might want to pull into a turnout to take pictures of the mounds of rocks and rubble abandoned along the banks by gold-fevered miners, like piles of dirty clothes. The view to the west up Sugar Creek, with the Russian Wilderness beyond, is also rather photogenic. After a few more bends of the boulder-bound road, you will top a slight rise and drift into Callahan.

Named for settler Mathias Bernard Callahan, the way station boasts a colorful past, explained on a highly-polished bronze panel set in an imitation boulder of white cement. For centuries this area, located at the junction of the East and South forks of Scott River, served as a meeting site for trading between the Shasta tribes of Scott Valley and Wintun Indians in the south. During the 1850s gold rush, moccasin-scuffed paths became trails deeply rutted by pack mules, hauling supplies over the mountain for miners. By 1854, the pack trails evolved into wagon roads for stagecoaches, hauling passengers between Oregon Territory and California.

A six-horse team was required to pull the coaches up out of the valley below, and travelers were then transferred to mules for the trip over Scott Mountain. Dusty in summer, muddy in the spring, it must have been one tough trek. When snow covered the passes, the road was kept open by oxen, and mule riders were transferred to sleighs. It wasn't until 1860 that the last six miles of road over the summit from the Trinity River were finished by the California Stage Company, eliminating the need for mules. Deemed safer from Indian raids than trails to the east, this old toll road fell to disuse after completion of the railroad in the Sacramento River Canyon in 1887.

There is plenty of space to park along the side of the highway in Callahan. (It's not exactly a Disneyland attraction.) As you walk the block of crumbling buildings, you might expect to hear a cacophony of sounds: the creak of wooden wheels, the bray of mules, the snort of horses, and the clamor of arriving travelers. How inviting the Callahan Ranch Hotel must have looked: a covered front porch as shelter from rain or snow, a two-story structure with seven windows across the front and a brick chimney at each end, promising fires on the hearths. Compare what you see today, porch roof sagging, windows missing, paint faded and peeling, with the Yreka Museum's brilliantly white, impeccable replica.

Next to the hotel is Scott Valley's oldest general store, the Harrington Store, its boardwalk crumpled, its metal roof buckled, and a wire fence in front to prohibit entry, a barely standing derelict, unrestored. Across the way stands an impressive two-story, cut-stone building, door and windows boarded up—no admittance. However, the Emporium next door is open to the few hundred souls inhabiting Callahan, and doing a brisk business. (What a marvelous candidate this hamlet would be for an historical restoration and preservation grant!)

As you leave the sad, almost ghost town behind, Highway 3 crosses the Scott River Bridge and begins its climb over Scott Mountain. A sign says "not advisable for autos with trailers," but drivers of mammoth RVs and pickups hauling boats ignore the words of caution. Along the way up the mountain, pause at a turnout on your left, even if it means a come-about for a look back. I can only hope that this incredible place will continue to welcome travelers, even those who might like to settle here. But please— citizens of Scott Valley—defy any attempt to build a freeway; deny urban sprawl, parking meters, shopping malls, and the ubiquitous Walmart. Keep your valley pure.

Despite the warning sign at the bottom of the grade, it's a fairly easy eight-mile drive up to the summit of Scott Mountain, the border between Siskiyou and Trinity counties. Here, the Pacific Crest Trail again crosses your path and you might hike a mile or two of the 120 miles of the Klamath National Forest segment. A small campground provides a resting place for those more vigorous hikers chugging along the 2600 miles between Mexico and Canada.

When you pull away from the wide, flat summit, the curves really begin, snaking their way down the mountain, tempting the driver to count them during the six-mile descent. At the foot of the grade, a less inviting road takes its paved but potholed, sometimes one-lane way, off to the northeast. This is the upper end of the Trinity Heritage Scenic Byway, a scraggly trail variously named International Paper Road, Parks Creek Road, and Forest Service Route 17. Following the Upper Trinity River, it twists and turns its way over the Trinity Divide between China Peak and Eddy Peak. Springs from these mountains form the headwaters of the Sacramento River on the eastern side and of the Trinity River on the west.

Whether or not you decide to make the thirty-some mile drive to the end of Route 17, at least park in the wide turnaround and walk over to the river. During the summer months, this narrow, rippling stream seems a feeble beginning for the broad, fast-moving river you traveled beside on Highway 299. Come spring, however, raging snowmelt waters flood the canyon, leaving piles of debris caught in the bankside boulders. At Bear Creek you will see evidence of the power of the water in flood stage: hillsides stripped bare, stream banks gouged with deep crevices, and remnants of trees left standing, like stark gray ghosts.

From this point, Highway 3 going south is bordered by the Klamath National Forest on the west and the Shasta National Forest on the east. The byway closely skirts the river, with several forest service campgrounds at water's edge and alternative loops tracing the old stage road. On the opposite hillside one can still see some blackened remains of the 1958 fire on Ramshorn Mountain. Winding eastward at the base, a gravel road leads 39 miles over the Trinity Mountains to Castella and I-5. Soon after passing the Trinity River campground, you catch your first really good look at the spiky crags comprising the Trinity Alps, a special photo-opportunity stop, with the highway curving ahead.

After another mile, turn right on Coffee Creek Road and turn right again on Derrick Flat Road to the forest service fire station. Even if it's closed, you can collect informative materials displayed in a rack on the outside wall. I frequently buy a sandwich in the deli of the Coffee Creek Store and hobnob with the locals at the picnic tables outside. A cleverly designed billboard, protected by a peaked roof, advertises Coffee Creek Village Innkeepers, with a map and the notation that brochures are available in the Country Store.

Also enjoyable is the drive west along the creek, passing the elementary school and an A-frame community church. I pulled into the circular driveway in front to take a peek inside and was greeted by the handyman, who turned out to be the pastor. He told me the church was built in the 1950s by the Seymour family, owners of all the land in the little valley at that time. When I asked about attendance, he admitted to 52 churchgoers the previous Sunday, nearly filling the tiny structure.

Five miles up Coffee Creek is Northern California's only 3-Diamond Dude Ranch, on the eastern side of the Trinity Alps Wilderness. The rustic but refined facilities are beautifully laid out: a swimming pool in front of the lodge, volleyball and badminton courts, a conference room and recreation room, cabins nestled in the woods, meadows and corrals across the creek. Limited to 50 guests weekly, the ranch offers a great variety of planned activities, including hayrides, horseback riding, and wilderness pack trips.

A mile south on Highway 3, I suggest a right turn on the Carrville Loop to wend your way slowly under ancient oaks along the route of the California-Oregon stage road, instantly obliterating 150 years. For the ultimate in gracious lodging, I can heartily recommend a stopover at the historic Carrville Inn. Built in the mid-1800s by James Carr and his wife Sarah, the original house was destroyed by fire in 1917 and rebuilt the following year with lumber milled on the ranch. Restoration of the neglected property was completed in 1988 and purchased by Dave and Sheri Overly.

Their efforts to create a bed-and-breakfast inn of the finest quality have been most successful. Wide verandahs with wicker rockers overlook sweeping lawns, an orchard, a swimming pool, a barn, chicken house and corrals, and peacocks mingling with llamas, horses, and a pig. Common rooms include a wood-paneled parlor with rock fireplace, a game room with a bar, and a large dining room with windows overlooking the garden. (After a fabulous breakfast, be sure to take the short trail uphill behind the inn to see the Carr family's little cemetery.)

If you feel the need for a more strenuous walk, ask about the road just a smidgen north of the inn, leading to the beginning of a trail that will take you into two wilderness lakes. From the end of the road, it's an easy two-mile hike to the deep, granite-walled Little Boulder Lake and the more shallow, lily-pad-covered Big Boulder Lake.

Another side-jaunt recommended by the Overlys is a visit to Alpen Cellars Winery. After leaving the Carrville Loop Road, watch for a sign with an arrow pointing east on the left side of Highway 3, at the junction of East Fork Road. The winery was established in 1984 by Mark Groves, who has lived in the area since he was a boy. He notes that it is a "family venture where each of us take part in the long painstaking process of wine production." Although it seems an unlikely location to grow wine grapes, his vintner son, Keith, produces award wining wines. Their Gewarztraminer was nominated first place in North America in 2001.

At this point, Highway 3 curves around the head of Trinity Lake, river water impounded by a dam some 20 miles south. the water is stored and diverted to provide irrigation for farmlands in the central valley. When the lake is low, the shore is lined with piles of rock and gravel, more leftovers from the gold rush. Stop at the North Shore Vista to read the interpretive sign explaining a mining process called dredging involving a barge with huge buckets that dug into a pond or river bottom to scoop up sludge. After gold flakes were extracted, the fine soil settled to the bottom and rocks were left piled along the banks.

You are now driving a major tourist route, the Trinity Unit of a National Recreation Area, cluttered with picnic areas, boat-launching ramps and boat-renting marinas, family-oriented resorts, forest service campgrounds, and parks for recreational vehicles. You will also notice that the amount of traffic definitely increases.

South on Highway 3, after crossing Swift Creek Bridge, jog left into Trinity Center—the town that traveled. Founded in 1851 as a center for trade along the stage route, it was moved for the first time in the late 1850s to make way for river dredging, and again 100 years later when that site was drowned by the lake. Drive around this little town to look for the few historical buildings, re-located before the dam was filled.

On the corner of Airport Road you will see The Sas-quatch Restaurant, with its statue of Bigfoot, and a quar-ter mile down the same road is the Scott Museum, open summer afternoons, Tuesday to Saturday. The airport features an annual Labor Day Fly-in B-B-Q, a benefit for the Lions Club community projects.

After leaving Trinity Center, this now not-so-scenic byway veers south by west on a long flat stretch of road, with views of the lake obscured by thick stands of trees. Keep a close watch for Covington Mill Road on the left, and turn and drive past the site of a lumber mill that cut the large beams used for construction of the mining dredges. A mile farther looms a magnificent four-story, to-

Bowerman Barn 1878

tally handcrafted barn with a foundation of cut stone, a frame of mortise and tenon joints covered with whipsawn pine boards attached with hand-forged nails. Built in 1878 by Jacob Bowerman, the barn is now on the National Register of Historic Places. A forest service brochure tells the story of the family who farmed the surrounding 160 acres and kept a way station for travelers on the Weaverville-Trinity Center Stage Road.

Nine miles after Covington Mill Road, Stuarts Fork River comes down from the west to flow into Trinity Lake. It was from this river that water was taken 29 miles by ditches and sluice boxes to power the hydraulic monitor seen along Highway 299 west of Weaverville. (Industrious and ingenious!)

As the road swings around the Stuarts Fork arm of the lake, I suggest another stop at the Osprey Information Center. Look for these fascinating birds perched on tree limbs above the lake, scanning the water for an unwary fish. The osprey's competitors are nine pairs of resident bald eagles, one of the largest nesting populations at any reservoir in California. They range in size from 30 to 40 inches tall, weigh 10 to 12 pounds, and have a wingspan up to seven feet. You can identify adult birds by their white head, neck, and tail, with yellow bill and legs. They fly with straight wings and do not hover. Osprey appear similar, with a white head and a dark band across the eyes, but they fly with bent wings and they do hover.

Just past this turnout, Highway 3 leaves the lake, goes up and over Slate Creek Divide for a couple of miles before scenic byway travelers should turn left on Trinity Dam Blvd., County Highway 105. After nine miles of winding road over Buckeye Ridge, you will come to Trinity Vista Point, with a picnic area and a deck providing a panoramic, picture-postcard view of the lake, the Trinity Alps and, if the air is clear, the snow-covered peak of Mt. Shasta in the distance.

Two miles farther south, pull into another turnout for an overlook of Trinity Dam, one of the tallest earth-filled dams in the world, 466 feet from bedrock to its half-mile-wide top. Completed in 1961, the dam encompasses 145 miles of shoreline. Below the dam, the highway closely follows the river as it gradually widens into Lewiston Lake. These waters are drawn from the bottom of Trinity Dam, then impounded behind Lewiston Dam, and diverted to flow through the Clear Creek Tunnel for 11 miles to a powerhouse, eventually dumping into Whiskeytown Lake.

Because speedboats aren't allowed on Lewiston, the lake provides a quiet place to fish, canoe, or kayak. If you are overnighting in one of several forest service campgrounds along the seven-mile stretch of riparian shoreline, a deer or gray fox might cross your campsite and a raccoon will surely rustle around the trash cans—if a bear doesn't get there first.

At the end of the lake and past the Lewiston Lake Vista Point below the dam, the highway crosses a new bridge over the tamed Trinity River. A left turn will take you up to a fish hatchery, built to compensate for the loss of upstream spawning habitat for salmon. After migrating upriver, fish are stripped of their eggs for artificial rearing. Operated by the California Department of Fish and Game, the hatchery welcomes visitors during weekday business hours to watch salmon leaping the fish ladder.

Return to the bottom of the hill, cross the highway to Deadwood Road, and follow it to Lewiston, one of the oldest settlements along the Trinity River. The town was named for B.F. Lewis, who operated the first ferry for pack horses traveling between Shasta and Weaverville. Now a National Historic Gold Mining Town, 13 structures from the mid-1800s are still in use.

You pass the Lewiston Hotel built in 1862 as a stagecoach stop, destroyed by fire in 1898, and rebuilt a year later. Although it no longer offers lodging, it is a fine place to dine, dinner only. Next to it is Old Lewiston Inn, a deck-lined, bed-and-breakfast overlooking the river. As well as the four rooms in this new section, there are three small rooms in the historic Baker House, built in 1875 as a private residence. Rumor says it hides a checkered past, an irate husband who shot his wife and her lover. I wonder if their ghosts haunt the place?

Deadwood Road dead-ends in the historic center of the old town. In this tiny crossroads village, you will discover a group of charming buildings nestled at the base of steep hills like treasures in a well-woven basket. Where the Lewiston Turnpike came down the hill to the river, there was a trading post called Dutch John's, later owned by Jacob Paulson. Today, The Country Peddlar occupies Paulson's mercantile, with its rusted metal roof, collection of old gas pumps on the front porch, and Trinity County's oldest known bar inside.

On the hill above is a one-room, red schoolhouse, originally The Sons of Temperance Hall, now the community library. Farther up the hill, you will see a miniature bit of New England, the white Congregational Church, its steeple blessing the souls of pioneers buried in the cemetery in front. The picket-fence enclosed, carefully tended gravestones date back to 1850.

LEWISTON

I must admit to a fondness for Lewiston. On my first visit after turning off Highway 299, had I followed Lewiston Dam Blvd., (now the newer part of town), I would have missed it altogether. However, I unknowingly turned left at a sign pointing to Old Lewiston and inched my van timidly down the very steep, narrow old turnpike to the bottom of the hill. Then I was confronted by a fragile-looking, one-lane structure in order to cross the river, which almost ended my visit before it began. However, after noting the warning sign "The first vehicle on has the right-of-way," I looked for oncoming traffic, took a deep breath and forged ahead. (I've since crossed it many times with no trepidation.)

It was a smart move. As I turned left on Rush Creek Road, another sign caught my attention, Old Lewiston Bridge RV Resort. Two brothers, Bill and Tom Miranda, have turned an old fish camp into a first-rate resort, and I have taken advantage of their hospitality on several occasions. As longtime residents of Lewiston, they made valuable suggestions for my explorations around the Trinity River country.

At this point in your journey, you have the option of driving northwest on Rush Creek Road to rejoin Highway 3, and turning left to return to Weaverville and the Trinity River Scenic Byway. Or, you can drive four miles south on Trinity Dam Blvd. back to Highway 299 and go east to I-5. If you decide to follow the scenic byways of Northeastern California, described in Part Two of this guide, you will travel from forested, river-carved canyons to volcanic uplifted plateaus—equally fascinating country.

PART TWO: NORTHEASTERN CALIFORNIA

Chapter VII
THE PEOPLE AND THE LAND

Jedediah Smith was not the only fur hunter to roam the rivers of California during the first quarter of the nineteenth century. His Canadian rivals, employees of the Hudson's Bay Company, also swarmed over the northwest territory. In 1829, one Alexander McLeod rode down the Shasta Valley on a trapping expedition, working the rivers as far south as present-day Stockton in the Sacramento River Valley.

By year's end, McLeod turned north, attempting to trap in the streams flowing from the mountains on the eastern side of the valley. He pushed his luck too far. Heavy snows forced him to cache precious furs, his horses perished, and McLeod staggered back to Fort Vancouver, only to be discharged from the company. Despite his disgrace, he has not been forgotten: McCloud River bears his moniker, and a mountain pass is named Dead Horse Summit for his horses.

Peter Skene Ogden dispatched his duties as a company man and expedition leader with a great deal more success. Described by his comrades as "short, dark and exceedingly tough, a fellow of good humor and infinite jest who traveled his trail with a smile," he obviously reveled in their esteem. Like Smith, he also kept a journal. Written on cured slabs of beaver skin, his notes later augmented his memoirs: *In 1829 I was appointed to explore the tract lying south of the Columbia, between that river and California. It was in the month of September that I bade adieu . . . with a party of thirty men to overcome the obstacles and encounter the perils which long experience had taught me to anticipate. We journeyed a month through a barren and sterile country before we came upon traces of any human inhabitants.*

To Ogden, the inhabitants were scarcely human. He wrote of atrocious and unprovoked cruelty practiced by the natives against those engaged in the fur trade. *Among the many losses, to us the unkindest cut of all was the death of an ass. Surely his sad end ought to be recorded, if it were only to show that the most harmless of all creatures have no security against the murderous intentions of the Indians in these wilds!* He apparently mourned the loss of a donkey more than the natives brought down by his gun.

In reading the account of Ogden's travels, and his opinion about the Indians, we must view his judgment in the context of his era. To our enlightened minds, we might view Ogden as the savage.

As the first trailblazer to traverse the intermountain-west from north to south, Ogden is credited with discovering the Humboldt River as a route across the Great Basin of present-day Nevada. Following this approach to the Sierra Mountains, he tracked the eastern slopes to the Colorado River, turned up the Sacramento Valley to the Pit River, and crossed northeastern California into Oregon. After circumventing the snow-covered peak he wrote: *There is a mountain equal in height to Mount Hood. I have named the mountain Shastise for the Shas-ti-ka Indians.*

Inevitably, tales about rich and fertile lands beyond the frontier, taken back to the Midwest by returning adventurers, fired every farmer's imagination. As early as 1831, a road agent who had never traveled farther west than St. Louis published a circular giving directions to *all Persons of Good Character who wish to Emigrate to the Oregon Territory.* His timing, if not his information, was perfect. The increasing scarcity of beaver pelts, and the decline of an international fur trade, had left trappers and traders adrift. Because they were intimately acquainted with every trail across the country, they proved to be excellent guides.

Such a guide should have been hired by 22-year-old Missourian, John Bidwell. Intent upon leading the first wagon train westward, he organized the Western Emigration Society. Scoffers proclaimed, "It is the most unheard of, foolish, wild goose chase that ever entered the brain of man." The taunt cast doubt in many minds. Of the 500 people who eagerly signed on, only 69 wagons left Missouri in May 1841. Bidwell later wrote: *Our ignorance of the route was complete. We knew only that California lay west.*

After joining a group of missionaries intent on saving native souls, they followed the Oregon Trail as far as Fort

Hall in Idaho. From there, Bidwell's group of 32 men, one woman and a child, swung south along the Humboldt River across the barren desert, survived an attack by Indians, abandoned their wagons, and loaded their possessions on mules, horses, and four oxen.

When they came face-to-face with the snowcapped Sierra peaks on October 28, Bidwell wrote: *If California lies beyond those mountains, we shall never be able to reach it.* With sheer guts and foolhardy courage, his party crossed the divide at Sonora Pass and pushed down the Stanislaus River into the valley. His naivete is mind-boggling, and his accomplishments even more so. He was elected to the senate of the new state of California, achieved the rank of General in the Civil War, and founded the town of Chico at the base of the Sierra Nevada foothills. The mansion built for him is now the Bidwell State Historic Park.

When it became obvious to the U.S. government that more precise information was needed for would-be emigrants, John Charles Fremont, a member of the Corps of Topographical Engineers, was commanded to lead a series of expeditions to survey and map the country from the Rocky Mountains westward. As had other pathfinders before him, he was seeking the mythical Buenaventura River, believed to flow from the Rockies across the Great Basin, through the Sierra Nevada to the bay of San Francisco. Each explorer, stumbling upon the Sacramento River, thought *this is it*: until they discovered it flowed from north to south rather than east to west.

In spite of this major disappointment, Fremont wrote: *My mission always lay in the opening up of unknown lands, the making of unknown countries known.* And this he accomplished with great flair, adding a literary quality to his scientific reports. Upon reaching the junction of two rivers, the Sacramento and the Pit, he caught his first glimpse of Mt. Shasta, and described it as *ascending like an immense column upward fourteen thousand feet, the summit glistening with snow.* His geographical accuracy and vivid descriptions, published as a government document in 1845, became the primary guidebook for thousands of pioneer settlers. As one historian wrote about Fremont: *He was a man of destiny—or at least a man who, seizing the coattails of expansion, would endeavor to make himself destiny's darling.*

Peter Lassen, a very different breed of man, appeared on the Western landscape in the mid-1800s. Danish born, he emigrated to America at age 29, settled for a spell in Missouri, traveled overland to Oregon 10 years later, and down the coast by boat to California. Naturalized by the Mexican governor of the state, by 1844 he had acquired a 22,000-acre Spanish Land Grant along the Sacramento River. His rancho, flour mill, and sawmill soon became a way station for John Bidwell, John Fremont, and Kit Carson.

Hoping to attract farmers to settle around his ranch, he made a journey back to the Midwest in 1847. As leader of a 12-wagon train contingent westward, he managed to get lost and wandered too far into the northern mountains. He finally turned south down the Pit River into the valley and home—too late. Gold had been discovered in the Sierra foothills and all his would-be settlers dashed up the river canyons, gold pans banging their backsides.

While researching Peter Lassen, my admiration for him grew. Considering the meager amount of geographical data available during his time, he didn't meander too far off base. (I've been known to get lost, in spite of the number of maps that always accompany me.) The man was respected by his peers, loved by the natives, and so revered by a nephew many generations removed, that Rene Lassen made several trips from Denmark to trace his life, and write a biography of Uncle Peter: *The Story of Peter Lassen and the Lassen Trail*. A county, a mountain peak, a national park, and a national forest are named for the adventurous man from Denmark—including Lassen's Trail, winding torturously up and around and through it all.

Of all the explorers of that time, Bidwell, Fremont, and Lassen seemed to be more in tune with the natives, and expressed more compassion for their plight. *They are,* Fremont wrote, *a race of people whose great and constant occupation was the means of procuring a subsistence.* He commented frequently on the abundance of salmon, acorns, elk, and deer available to the Shasta and the so-called Pit River Indians, the Achomawi, and Atsugewi.

The degree of sophistication attributed by the whites to the natives revolved around their clothing—or absence of it. This too, depended upon the materials available; skin from sea creatures or land animals, feathers from birds or coverings woven from plant fibers, the inner bark of trees or tule rushes. Shelter varied from rectangular structures of hand-hewn planks to circular cones of slabs of bark, some covered with earth or thatch.

The topographical map of northeastern California reads like a biography of these first peoples: natives, trappers, explorers, and settlers. Rough country, tough people. Today, the names of many rivers and forests, valleys and mountain peaks pay them homage. Their major travel route and lifeline was the great central valley, closed on the northwest by the forested Klamath Mountains, on the east by the volcanic Cascade Range, and at the southern end of the Cascades, the Sierra Nevada Mountains, a 400-mile-long granite wall, uplifted by countless earthquakes. East of the Cascades and the Sierra, spreading like a vast sagebrush steppe, are the Modoc Plateau and the Great Basin's high desert. All of them challenges to be conquered.

Encompassed within these northeastern hinterlands are five of California's 18 national forests: a small portion of the Klamath National Forest, nearly two million acres of the Modoc, a section of the Shasta, all named for native tribes, one-million plus acres of Lassen National Forest, named after Peter Lassen, and the slightly larger Plumas National Forest named by a wandering Spaniard, who thought the river running through it looked like feathers, hence *plumas*.

Several biologically unique areas, tucked within these forests, have been granted wilderness protection: The largest of these are 21,000 acres around Buck's Lake in Plumas National Forest; the 42,000-acre Ishi Wilderness, ancestral homeland of the Yahi Yana tribe in the Lassen National Forest; and the 38,000-acre wilderness that surrounds Mount Shasta. One of the two major volcanoes that dominate the north country, Mt. Shasta rises 4000 feet above its rival, Mt. Lassen. Other, smaller wilderness areas are located within Lava Beds National Monument and Lassen Volcanic National Park.

Three National Wildlife Refuges around Tule Lake, Lower Klamath Lake, and along the remote Butte Valley in northeastern California protect all manner of wild creatures. First established in 1903, the designation prohibited hunting and trapping, a prohibition that was amended in 1950 to permit such activities on some refuges, an amendment that has resulted in a great deal of nationwide controversy.

Two major rivers flow through northeastern California: the McCloud River runs through a small portion of southern Siskiyou County, and angles south through Shasta County to feed into the Sacramento River; the Pit River, the longest in northeastern California, angles diagonally from its headwaters in the Warner Mountains to also join the Sacramento River.

Three highways traversing the country east of I-5 have been designated scenic byways, and you will follow them in Part Two of this guide. They include 100 miles of the Modoc Volcanic Scenic Byway and 170 miles of the Lassen Volcanic Scenic Byway. The latest route to be awarded the National Forest Service coveted designation is the 180-mile Shasta Volcanic Scenic Byway. The aim is to provide a link between the chain of volcanoes running through the Cascades of Oregon and California.

The first time I drove Peter Ogden's *barren and sterile country*, its isolation from civilization both appalled and enthralled me. But as I researched the highways penetrating this remoteness, I discovered previously unexplored fields of study that made the journey not only imperative but rewarding. Even though we can't observe these hinterlands with the eyes of Ogden or Fremont, we can try to imagine the potential they envisioned and appreciate their efforts to guide us.

MODOC VOLCANIC SCENIC BYWAY

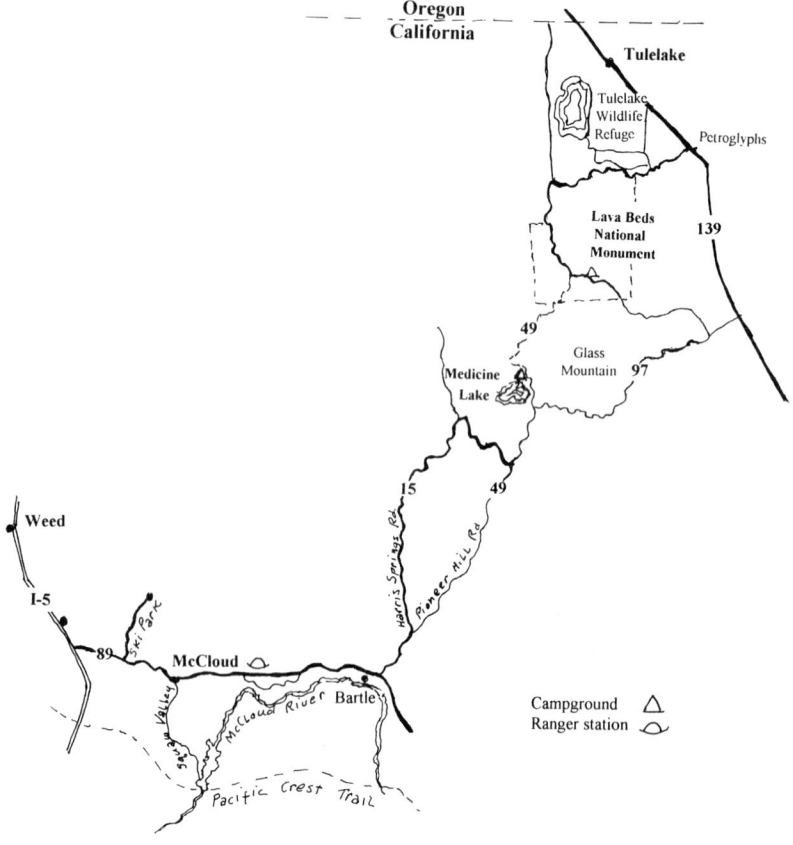

Chapter VIII
MODOC VOLCANIC SCENIC BYWAY
California State Highway 89,
Forest Service Routes 15 & 49
100 Miles

The gateway to the scenic byway that rises to a chaotic jumble of lava begins at the southern base of the mountain Peter Ogden named Shastise, for the Shas-ti-ka Indians. The native tribes of Northern California have always held the mountain in reverence and respected its power. John Muir, tramping around Mt. Shasta 30 years after Ogden, agreed that *the colossal cone rising in solitary grandeur might well be regarded as an object of religious worship.* Today, Mt. Shasta still exerts a magnetic force, drawing New Age spiritual seekers up its labyrinth of trails to chant or meditate.

In his role as a naturalist, John Muir added that the mountain represented the *last feeble expression of the mighty power that lifted the entire mass . . . from the volcanic depths far below the surface of the plains.* Although considered a dormant volcanic system, hot springs bubble up from its depths, and earthquakes rumble along its fault lines. Yet for centuries, undaunted explorers have looked to the snowcapped peak, towering above the slopes, as a beacon, guiding the way. As we do today, traversing I-5, California's north-south axis.

For our exploration of the country, we will leave the Interstate and head east on Highway 89 toward McCloud. After 10 miles of gentle uphill driving, you ascend Snowman's Hill Summit, gaining 1000 feet in elevation. If you are a winter-sports fan, or are looking for a variety of summer activities, make a left at Ski Park highway. You can ride the chairlift to the top, go mountain biking, or rock climb on a state-of-the-art tower, and dine on the lodge's patio.

Return to the highway and drive another mile to McCloud, make a left turn on West Colombero Drive, cross the railroad tracks, and turn right on Main Street. I suggest you park in the lot in front of the train depot, take a deep breath of champagne air, and a long look at Mt. Shasta to the north. If ever a town was blessed with a fantastic view, this is it—stunningly photogenic!

Settled by the McCloud River Lumber Company during the 1890s, it remained a company-owned town until 1965. Rows of small, cookie-cutter houses for the workers border the side streets, and magnificent mansions of company managers dot the hillsides above—several of them reincarnated as bed-and-breakfast inns. The railway, built to provide cheap transportation for timber brought down from the mountains, now offers one-hour, open-air excursions in something that looks like a cattle car. For a more comfortable, and exclusive ride, you can make reservations for the Shasta Sunset Dinner Train, running evenings during the summer.

McCloud has become the ultimate tourist town, and you need to stroll the streets of this impeccably maintained village to appreciate its ambiance. Take a short walk north back to Colombero Drive, and turn right to pass the Stoney Brook Inn built in 1922, now a retreat and conference center. Turn right again to walk south on Main to take a gander at the bright yellow McCloud Hotel across from the railway station. Built in 1915, and now a Nationally Registered Historic Landmark, it provides elegant four-star-rated lodging for dinner-train passengers.

As you drift down Main, you will pass an Italian restaurant, the post office, the railroad office in the bank building, and the Heritage Junction Museum—all worthy of a visit. Across the way, drop into the white, dormer-windowed Mercantile Building, a general store that will take you on a nostalgic trip into the past. You might be tempted to splurge in the candy cupboard, or have a cup of coffee and sweet roll in the corner cafe.

Touring the streets around Old Town, you will notice that McCloud is also a mecca for square dancers, who swing their partners in another restored structure on the corner of Broadway and Pine. For golfers, the McCloud Golf Course, the first nine-holer in Northern California, is located on Squaw Valley Road, down a mile or so from Highway 89. Campers congregate in the Dance Country RV Park on the corner of Highway 89 and Squaw Valley Road. My usual choice for camping is Friday's RV Retreat six miles farther down the road, which ends at McCloud Lake—a good fishing spot, or so I've been told.

If you are an avid hiker, the Squaw Valley Creek Trail is the one to explore. Just past the RV park, turn right on a dirt road, drive three miles, and cross a concrete bridge to the trailhead parking lot. Although five miles long, it is an easy walk along a beautiful stream, shaded by a conifer forest. It even joins the Pacific Crest Trail before it forks off and heads uphill.

As you return to Highway 89 and head east, be sure to stop at the ranger station on Forest Road to gather leaflets about shorter hikes and driving tours. You will be given directions for the six-mile McCloud River Loop, leading to waterfalls and beautiful scenic trails. Drive five miles from town, turn south off the highway at the sign for Fowler's Camp, and park in the forest service maintained turn-around at Lower Falls. Riverside paths lead to Middle and Upper Falls, providing waterfall overlooks, access to swimming beaches, and picnic areas.

From the parking lot, you can continue on the McCloud River loop road to Highway 89, or return the way you came, and turn east on the highway. If you intend to follow the Modoc Volcanic Scenic Byway into this very remote portion of northeastern California, there are some preparations you should make. While at the ranger station, ask for the "Self-Guided Roadside Geology Tour of the Medicine Lake Highlands." It will be invaluable in making choices along the route.

Elevations are high and, even in the summer, the weather can chill rapidly. Take along warm clothing as well as sturdy walking shoes. Dining facilities and lodging possibilities, other than camping, are sparse and simple. So, before leaving this enclave of civilization, stock up on water and snacks, and a full tank of fuel. From McCloud, drive about 10 miles to Bartle, a small lodge and cafe on the south side of the road. Watch for the byway sign, and turn left on Route 15, a U.S. Forest Service Primary Route. Your destination is Medicine Lake and Lava Beds National Monument.

After four miles, pull into a turnout at the junction of Route 15, Harris Springs Road, and Route 49, the Powder Hill Road. It is at this point that you will need to make a decision—and it is confusing. The routes do not appear on the official California tourist map, and on the AAA California state map, only one road is shown, but not numbered. If you are following the larger, more detailed AAA map of Northern California, both routes are named and numbered. (Neither is open in the winter.) Route 15 carries the designation of Modoc Volcanic Scenic Byway. Since I have driven both roads, the selection of Route 15 as "the most scenic" is difficult for me to understand. If you picked up the *Roadside Geology Tour Guide*, the decision is yours.

On the mid-June day that I drove the highways, the vision that came to mind was of driving from the tail end of a humpback whale, curving up the backbone to the blowhole, its barnacle-crusted flanks sloping away on each side. So very few cars, trucks, or campers passed me, the feeling created was of isolation and solitude. Long gone is the roar of vented fire, the hiss of steam, the rumble blasts of boulders from the volcano above. The scarcity of highway signs intensified the notion of being "back of the beyond"—a phrase mysterious and beguiling.

What will you see if you opt to follow Route 15? Six miles past the junction, a dry lake bed lies off to the right, glimpsed only through the pines. Four miles beyond, the turnoff for Harris Springs campground, and nine miles farther, a red-rock lava flow and a red cinder cone—both a mile off the main road. After another four miles, you need to bear right to reach Medicine Lake by following seven miles of unpaved pumice road with a warning sign: "It is very easy to get stuck in pumice."

If you decide to follow Route 49, you will climb an escarpment that resulted from an upthrust block of rock, a jumbled field of lava that spewed out of a giant crater, 10 miles northward. As the route continues up the sides of extinct volcano cones, the road side is bordered by stunted, gnarly Ponderosa pine and incense cedar, tenaciously rooted in the rocks. Unpaved side roads wander off to natural bridges, lava tubes, and ice caves.

After an elevation gain of 3,000 feet, you will reach the Medicine Lake Highlands, a result of the largest shield volcano in the Cascade Range blowing its top. Molten magma burst from several vents, and spread like an opening fan for miles below its base. Three miles past the junction where Route 97 butts into Route 49, turn west to Medicine Lake. Intensely blue, cloud-reflecting water fills the crater, created after the center of the volcano collapsed. As you drive around the lake, you will find lodgepole pine shaded campgrounds along the north shore, and boat-launch sites, day-use sandy beaches, and picnic areas on the southern shore.

Since the scenic byway continues 15 miles to the Lava Beds National Monument, it is at this point that I need to add a cautionary note. If you follow Route 49, you will drive eight miles on a paved, one-lane road with narrow turnouts, and then seven miles on a gravel, washboard,

dusty road to the paved route that leads through the monument. Envisioning my camper meeting a large motor home, I opted for an alternative but longer and safer route by driving three miles south back to Route 97 and heading east.

After five miles, there is a scenic turnout on the right side of the road, offering a distant view of Lassen Peak. As you proceed, you might also catch a glimpse of Glass Mountain to the north, a huge mass known for its black obsidian which sparkles in shafts of sunlight. After another 15 miles, watch for Route 10 leading nine miles northwest to the monument entrance. It is paved but a bit rough, so proceed slowly to avoid potholes in the asphalt.

Your first stop, of course, should be the visitor center to gather information for touring the park: a detailed map showing turnouts, picnic areas, and unpaved roads; a schedule of ranger-guided walks, cave tours, and campfire programs; flyers describing craters and cinder cones, caves, and bats. A small museum offers a wealth of books, photos and posters, and displays of Indian and geological artifacts.

A fact sheet describes places you can explore on your own, but be advised: side roads are dirt and gravel, deeply rutted, and covered with powdered pumice. You need to carry water at all times, and wear rugged hiking boots; trails over lava are bumpy, sharp, and slippery. If you plan to explore the caves, a hard hat is desirable, and a flashlight is essential. (They can be acquired at the ranger station.) There are no lodging or dining facilities throughout the park, but there is a forest service campground across the highway from the visitor center.

Declared a national monument by President Coolidge in 1925, the ten-mile-long by eight-mile-wide mesa formation on the north slope of the Medicine Lake shield volcano is probably visited by fewer tourists than any other national park in the country. Other than the forest service roads just described, the only way to reach it is by Highway 139 that runs through Modoc County on the east and leads to Klamath Falls, Oregon.

If this is your first adventure in what the natives termed "the land of burnt out fires," be prepared for a lunarscape by nature's abstract artist gone wild. Black molten strands of lava have congealed into distorted sculptures, or into smoothly arched bridges. Reddish piles of rock surround cinder cones, heaped on top of subterranean caves and tubes, formed when the molten core drained away. Juniper bushes bend and twist, as if trying to escape the wind.

If it all seems a barren wasteland, you might be startled by the flap of wings bursting from a thicket of brush, creatures scuttling among the rocks, or by a deer leaping across the road. Among the crumpled heaps of dark gray lava, you may see splattered bits of color: purple sage, feathery white rabbitbrush, spiky pink fireweed blossoms, and red Indian paintbrush. The most vivid colors and crystal pillar formations are to be found within the caves, along with frozen rivulets of ice.

Since most caves are holes in the ground with ladders descending into total darkness (and the claustrophobic feeling of crawling about is not for me), I opted for a brief look into the Mushpot Cave. Conveniently located in the visitor center parking lot, it is the only cave that is lighted and will give you a good introduction to exploring others. After driving the one-way, cave-loop road south from the parking lot, I decided one experience was enough. I much prefer hikes above ground in fresh air, with views more distant than the end of my flashlight's beam.

On my first night in the park, I camped at Indian Well Campground, where I was serenaded by a chorus of coyotes, and awakened refreshed and raring to go. My first leg-stretching hike was the one-mile Bunchgrass trail, an easy stroll along an old roadbed around Crescent Butte. A hearty breakfast (all campers' breakfasts should be hearty) invigorated me enough to tackle the uphill stretch to Schonchin Butte Lookout, named for a Modoc chief. The panoramic scene of layer upon layer of lava flows, high bluffs, and shelves of black rock, with the tip of Mt. Shasta shining beyond, was more breathtaking than the climb.

As I slowly followed the road through the park, I pulled over at every turnout, consulted the map, and read the interpretive signs at each weird formation. The description of Fleener Chimney attracted my attention, and I turned left to drive to the picnic tables nestled among junipers—just in time for lunch. The sign there told me this unusual 50-foot-deep hole was formed by a spatter cone spewing out globs of lava, leaving a natural chimney soaring above ground.

LAVA BEDS   JUNIPER

From that point, the route curves upward to run for a couple of miles along the top of a bluff, labeled the Devil's Homestead Lava Flow. For an inveterate history buff such as I, the next three turnouts were the most fascinating (and the saddest) section of the entire monument. The sites involved events in the so-called Modoc War between the Indians and the U.S. army.

Three decades after John Fremont wended his way up the Pit River, and three years before General Custer met his demise on the Big Horn River, trouble seethed between the Modocs and the settlers invading their land. Naturally, orders came for the offending Modocs to be transported to a reservation on the other side of the Oregon border, and, naturally, a defiant group of natives rebelled. The story of the band of 50 renegades hiding out for four bitterly cold winter months in the lava tubes, holding off 600 soldiers, is a chilling tale, with the end result inevitable.

Because I believe one of the essential pleasures of travel lies in discovery, I am leaving the interpretation of the Modoc War for you to discover on your own. Perhaps you will share my admiration for their leader Kientpoos, called Captain Jack by the whites and mourn the inability of two cultures to understand, and accept one another. A half-mile trail winds around Captain Jack's Stronghold, a natural fortress in lava tubes deep underground, with interpretive signs describing the battle,

Now, another decision needs to be made, depending upon the time of day, your capacity for downloading knowledge, and your level of energy. Although you are only a bit over 100 miles from McCloud, after spending the day wandering this gigantic geological and historical outdoor museum, you may say "enough is enough." But if you are inspired to explore farther, continue due east for another 12 or 15 miles to investigate Petroglyph Point.

The sides of this cinder cone that once rose as an island in the middle of Tule Lake are covered with circles and lines carved into the soft rock by natives crossing the water in canoes. Today, due to the draining of lake waters, the site is left high and dry. Unlike other tribes, the Modocs did not depict animals or humans, but devised a series of symbols with their own hidden meanings. A brochure is available that attempts to help you understand the significance of the site, but it also represents a dispute. Because of modern-day graffiti, a chain-link fence was put up to discourage scratchers, then taken down when the locals objected.

Unless you decide to follow Highway 139 to the town of Tulelake to seek overnight lodgings, backtrack to follow the road that skirts the southern shore of the Tule Lake National Wildlife Refuge. It was a late afternoon near sundown that I drove the route, pulling into the overlooks. Swirls of tule fog clung to stalks of cattails lining the murky bank, effectively cloaking nests tucked within their protection. A faint breeze raised a damp, musky odor from the swamp, and a tiny marsh wren flew from her hiding place. The kittering call of a bald eagle flying high above, and the flash of a white head, tinted pink in the

last bit of sunray, sent down its warning sign. Nature's battle, pitting one species against another, symbolizes the controversy surrounding the refuges—the constant struggle between environmentalists' desire to protect dwindling wildlife and the farmers' need for croplands to protect their livelihood. We will delve into this dispute in the next chapter—if you are still with me!

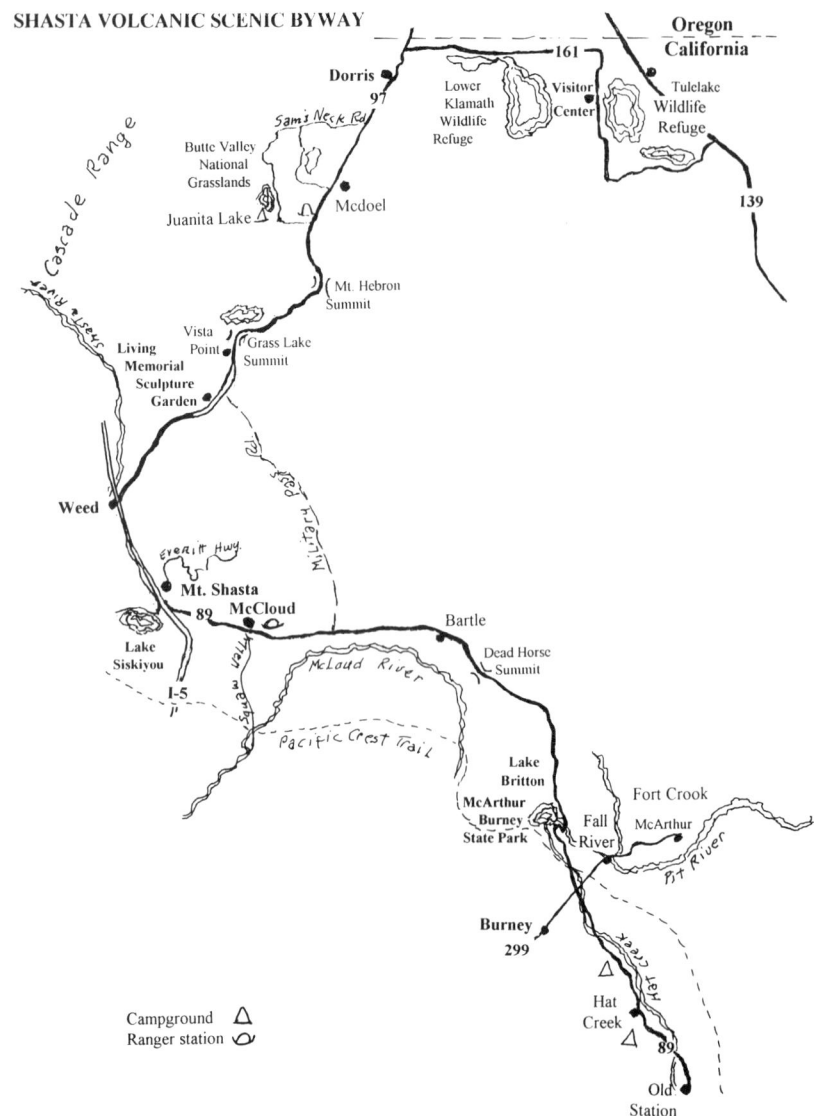

Chapter IX
SHASTA VOLCANIC SCENIC BYWAY
California Highway 161, U.S. Highway 97, California Highway 89
180 Miles

As you begin your journey along the northern border of California, visualize the expanse of shallow lakes and marshes that once spread over an immense basin on the eastern slope of the Cascade Mountains. Fill that mental image with massive flocks of migrating birds, lured to the wetlands as a flyway stopover or a nesting ground. The wetlands are dependent upon the whims of nature: lakes flooding during spring snowmelt, and marshes drying out in the summer months.

In an attempt to control these erratic changes, the U.S. Bureau of Reclamation devised a plan in 1905 to drain the swamps to extend the soil suitable for farming. The result should have been predictable. As wetland habitat diminished, the numbers of wildlife also decreased. Three years later, President Theodore Roosevelt, an avid outdoorsman, established the first wildlife refuge within the Klamath Basin, altogether establishing three each in California and Oregon.

Was it Rachel Carson, writing *Silent Spring* in 1962, who increased the country's awareness of the dangers of reclamation? *The preservation of wildlife and wildlife habitat means also the preservation of the basic resources of the earth, which men as well as animals must have in order to live.* As if alerted by her concern, the National Forest Service created a program during the 1970s and 80s to restore the last remnants of historic wetlands .

But the following decade brought several years of severe drought, creating a water shortage crisis that threatened farmers and environmentalists alike. The latest plan, coordinated by the Fish and Wildlife Service and the Bureau of Reclamation, is to flood parts of the refuges to keep waterfowl alive and to drain other parts for croplands, on a rotating basis. The kicker is that the water is drawn from the Klamath River for both projects, bringing forth howls of protest from downriver fisherfolk.

I can't help but wonder if alternating dry years with floods is nature's way of retaliation for mankind's messing with the weather cycles. An essayist whose name I have forgotten wrote: *Every so often it's nature's turn.* William Kittridge, an unforgettable Western writer, came of age turning wetlands into farmlands just over the border in Oregon. As did all ranchers in his day, he used chemicals to eliminate pests—until he was stunned by the silence. No more birdsongs filled the air. *Water birds are a metaphor for abundance*, he wrote, *life sustaining for the natives, the pioneer rancher, the sheep herder and the chuckwagon cook.*

All this and more you will learn if you drive five miles west of Tulelake to the Klamath Basin Wildlife Refuge headquarters and visitor center on Hill Road. Materials available there help to clarify the management plan for farming, fishing, and hunting within the refuge. Colorful exhibits illustrate the species of wildlife protected, and a plethora of handouts aid in their identification.

The refuge has developed an amazing educational program, as I discovered when I pulled into the parking lot, a big yellow school bus on my tail. Children of all sizes tumbled out, chirping like a flock of magpies. Rounded up by their adult leaders, they hiked up a steep trail to a hilltop lookout, the boldest ones dashing ahead, the littlest ones lagging behind.

Taking advantage of their absence, I slipped into the visitor center to make my quiet inspection of the displays. The receptionist explained the complex system of levee roads that crisscross the refuge, the numbered posts along the route correlating with tour guide pamphlets, the blinds or shelters set up for photographers, and the two-mile canoe channel winding around Tule Lake. (Reservations are necessary, binoculars most helpful; sunscreen, bug repellent, and drinking water are imperative.)

I also learned that the largest population of bald eagles in North America is concentrated in this particular area, with the winter months the best time to observe them. When I told the lady at the desk about the one I had seen the day before, she said there are resident eagles, and apparently I had lucked out. I hoped the children would spot them, but feared their constant chatter would frighten all wildlife away. (One of the distinct advantages of traveling solo!)

To continue your trip along the scenic byway, drive north on Hill Road four miles to Highway 161 and turn west, skirting the southern border of Oregon. The pale blue mirage of Upper Klamath Lake stretches away to the north, and its tag-end remnant, Lower Klamath Lake, fills a small basin on the south. Again, I parked in an overlook and left the van to walk, look, and listen. After the silence and solitude of the lava beds, this was a symphony in comparison, rising above lazy laps of water slurping among the reeds. The rustle of my footsteps disturbed a family of mallards, mama duck's tawny head nudging her chicks to safety. As I knelt down to look for the nest, a gull flew overhead, and swooped low to scold me for my invasion. For some strange reason, his sharp squawk reminded me of a ditty learned in a natural environment class long ago: *sedges have edges, rushes are round, grasses have nodes, and willows abound.*

Birdwatching has never been one of my special hobbies, but I was sorely tempted during that trip to add it to my list of interests. Dedicated birders should plan their visits to the refuges during early spring to witness white clouds of snow geese flying north, or in the fall to spot the double breasted cormorants, herons, and osprey.

Fifteen miles after leaving Hill Road, Highway 161 ends at Highway 97, the major route between I-5 and Klamath Falls, Oregon. As you turn south, you will notice an increase in traffic, but the drive is oddly serene. Originally, Butte Valley provided summer hunting grounds for the Modocs, but when the natives were vanquished in 1864, the country was sectioned into 160-acre homesteads. Farmers, ranchers, and stockmen moved in, meadows were plowed and planted with potatoes, and lakes were drained for open rangeland for cattle and sheep.

A funny thing happens when paradise is discovered. In 1907, the Southern Pacific Railroad decided to run their rails right up the middle of the valley, and now Highway 97 runs in tandem. At the upper end, the town of Dorris, a pleasant village of about 1000 inhabitants, certainly rates a visit. As the highway tops a slight rise and slants downhill to become Main Street, an RV park nestles under the trees on the right. Below and on the left is a market, a couple fast-food places, and a gas station.

I've been told that Primo Pizza is the best place for a meal, but I haven't tried it. If the Chamber of Commerce, on the corner of Main and Third, is open, you might inquire about dining and lodging facilities. Across the street, a little park gives place of honor to the world's largest flagpole, 200-feet tall, flying the stars-and-stripes, measuring 60 by 30 feet.

Between Dorris and Macdoel, 10 miles downwind, the Butte Valley National Grassland rolls out its green carpet. In an effort to reclaim overplowed and overgrazed substandard soils, the entire area was sown with wheatgrass. Flooding the grain fields after harvesting brings hunters from afar, intent on bagging their quota of waterfowl, ducks and geese, and upland game birds, quail and pheasant. Hunting seasons, bag limits, and regulations change every year and are established by the California Department of Fish and Game (see appendix).

Stop at the Goosenest Ranger Station a mile or so beyond Macdoel for more information on the Grasslands project and suggestions for a driving tour. If you follow the directions, you will wind past Juanita Lake with a campground (open summers only), a 1.5 mile paved nature trail, restrooms, and picnic tables, all accessible to the handicapped. The road then circles around the Butte Valley wildlife area and rejoins Highway 97.

Heading south again, the route curves up a thousand feet to Mt. Hebron Summit and dips down to the Grass Lake rest stop on the right side of the highway. As do all CalTrans rest stops, this one also offers billboards loaded with information about the country you are driving through. I pulled into the next vista point on Grass Lake Summit, which gives a wide-range view of Shasta Valley, unfolding like an open fan curving northward. Formed by a landslide when the north flank of the ancient Mt. Shasta volcano collapsed, Shasta Valley is speckled with small buttes, leftover rounded blocks of the old mountain.

The peaks of Mt. Shasta that you see today are a result of a series of eruptions which formed several overlapping cones. Each blast sent heaps of rocks down its flanks, building up deep deposits on the valley floor to create high plateaus. Between eruptions, snow and ice form glaciers in the crevices that feed a multitude of streams which disappear in the porous layers of lava and reappear as springs gushing from the rocky slopes. When glaciers melt during heavy rains or warm spells, mudflows coursing down the creek beds create the greatest threat to the communities built around the base of the mountain, but a lesser threat than another eruption would be.

At this point along the route, I wondered about the absence of scenic byway signs. Joanne Steele of the Siskiyou County Visitor Bureau, kindly provided the answer. The highways around Mt. Shasta received official designation as a Forest Service Scenic Byway in 2001, an interim step to gaining national status from the Federal Highways Administration as an All American Road. To qualify for this prestigious award, a route must be more than regionally scenic. It must include significant features in at least two out of six categories of national interest: archaeological, cultural, historical, natural, recreational, and scenic. Shasta Volcanic Scenic Byway qualifies in all six.

Only three other highways in California have achieved nationwide recognition: Yosemite and Death Valley as National Scenic Byways, and Big Sur's Route 1 as an All American Road. When the process is completed, Shasta Volcanic Scenic Byway will be a part of the volcanic legacy extending from Crater Lake in Oregon, through Lava Beds National Monument to Lassen Volcanic National Park. Byway signs have been put on hold until the nomination is accepted. Perhaps by the time you are traveling through, signs will be in place.

Descending the hill from the summit, the highway surprisingly widens into four lanes. Watch for the entrance to the Living Memorial Sculpture Garden on the right. Behind a rock-mounted sign, a gaunt, 12-foot-tall metal

MT. SHASTA

LIVING MEMORIAL SCULPTURE GARDEN

statue, the Peaceful Warrior, raises an arm in greeting. As you drive into the parking area, an information booth and a list of sponsors is on your left, and at the end, the names of veterans are inscribed on a marble Memorial Wall. Pathways like spokes in a wheel lead to groups of overpowering figures. Its hub, *The Why Group* was created by Dennis Smith, a Marine Corp veteran, whose declared purpose *is to uplift, edify and educate.* Located on leased forest service land within groves of newly planted pines, with Mt. Shasta in the background, the setting of the memorial is majestic.

I purposely haven't described the magnificent views of the mountain as seen from Highway 97. It gradually appears on the horizon, looming larger and larger. Mentioned by every explorer and settler venturing West, wagon tracks once circled the mountain's perimeter. The highway more or less parallels one of the earliest routes, the Yreka Emigrant Trail, a cutoff from the Applegate Trail. Two miles north of the sculpture garden on the south side of the highway, a bronze plaque, set in place by a volunteer organization, Trails West, Inc., relates the history. In 1846, the Applegate brothers pioneered a route from the Humboldt River across the northeastern corner of California and around Tule Lake into Oregon. The Yreka Trail offered a shortcut into the Shasta Valley.

Near the marker, Highway 97 is joined by the Military Pass Road, a route used by Lieutenant George Crook as he led his troops north on an Indian control mission in the 1850s (before he became a general in the Civil War). Unpaved and deeply rutted, the road offers those with four-wheel drive unusual sightings of the eastern side of Mt. Shasta, as it heads south for 32 miles to connect with Highway 89 east of McCloud.

At the end of Highway 97, on the right, there is a forest service fire station with a small rest area and picnic tables. Here, I suggest you temporarily ignore I-5 traffic nearby and drive into Weed. Established as a lumber town in the late 1800s, it is (as I say time and again about these northern California towns) worth a visit. The Chamber of Commerce, housed in a log cabin under the huge arch proclaiming the town's name, will gladly offer information about dining and lodging facilities, and will provide directions to the College of the Siskiyous, the golf course, and a 100-year-old mineral springs spa resort.

Your next destination is the town of Mount Shasta, 10 miles south of Weed via the Interstate. On the east looms Black Butte, a steep, treeless dome of very thick magma that rose from a crater at the base of Mt. Shasta about 10,000 years ago. A trail to the summit of Black Butte leads from Everitt Memorial Parkway, a 14-mile-drive winding 4,000 feet up the southwest flank of the mountain. The Parkway provides access to several trailheads and, as with all trails within the Mt. Shasta wilderness area, hiking permits are required and can be obtained at the ranger district station at 204 W. Alma Street.

Mount Shasta has been described as an alpine village, a town of boutiques and art galleries, fine restaurants, motels, and B&Bs. It is also a center for alternative health products, for retreats at mineral springs, and for wellness seminars and workshops. From I-5, take the central town exit to Lake Street, drive two blocks east to Pine, and turn left. The visitor center is on the corner and is your best source for all local information, including a downtown walking map.

If you are an Interstate shunner, and would like a more leisurely drive between Weed and Mount Shasta, I can recommend the Old Stage Road that winds south along the base of the Eddy Mountains through Strawberry Valley. During the heyday of stagecoaches, a hamlet sprouted on the west side of the valley, acquiring the Berryvale post office and a postmaster named Sisson. When Central Pacific laid its tracks on the eastern side, the town site and railroad station were given the name of Sisson, a name that stuck until 1924 when it was changed to Mount Shasta. The Sisson Museum is located just off Old Stage Road on Hatchery Lane near the fish hatchery.

Where the old road branches off to the left, stay on Barr Road to pass the Mount Shasta Resort (golf, tennis, lodging, and restaurant) to the Box Canyon Dam that creates Lake Siskiyou. Barr Road continues on around the southern arm of the lake to Lake Siskiyou Camp Resort. This is a splendid place to vacation, with camping sites on roads that circle up and around the hillsides. The resort also provides full hookup spaces, a swimming beach and boat ramp, picnic areas, a store, and the Howlin' Hound Restaurant. (Hint: Site 177 on the outside edge of Coyote Circle has a great view of Mt. Shasta.)

If you have taken this side jaunt, you will need to backtrack to Mount Shasta and the Interstate, and take the off-ramp for Highway 89. This will take you to McCloud, where the Modoc Volcanic Scenic Byway begins. Almost immediately after leaving town, the highway crosses Mud Creek, an example of a glacier-fed mudflow mentioned earlier in this chapter. In August 1924, deposits of sediment built up to a depth of 15 feet, overflowing into the McCloud River. In a couple more miles, the Military Pass Road, rounding the eastern side of Mt. Shasta from Highway 97, joins Highway 89.

Continue south past Bartle to ascend Dead Horse Summit, supposedly named to acknowledge Alexander McLeod's loss of horses and furs in the winter of 1829. After driving about 15 miles through thin stands of Ponderosa pines, Lake Britton fills a canyon on your right. Created when the Pit River was harnessed behind a Pacific Gas & Electric dam, there are ramps for boat launching, day-use picnic tables, and a sandy beach for swimming.

As the highway bends around the lake and crosses the Pit River, watch for the entrance gate on the right to McArthur-Burney Falls Memorial State Park. If you visit this park during the summer, you may feel that 564 acres is not enough to contain all the people—it is that close to civilization and that popular. During spring or fall, it is a place of pure delight. Just past the entrance station, pull into the parking area and hike the half-mile headwaters trail along the top of layers of basalt. Rainwater and snowmelt, retained in huge underground natural reservoirs and numerous springs, emerge in a double cataract to plunge 129 feet down to a deep pool at the base. Another mile-long nature trail winds down to the base of the falls beside moss-covered cliffs, accompanied by the roar from the falls, where darting swifts and swallows forage for insects.

The park is named for the valley's first settlers, Samuel Burney and the McArthurs, whose descendants gifted the property to the state in 1920. It is open year-round and provides campsites shaded by California black oaks and Oregon white oaks. It has a store for basic supplies. Since the Pacific Crest Trail wends its way down Burney Creek Canyon and through the park, some of the folks you encounter may be carrying heavy packs on their backs.

More substantial lodging than a tent, or more elegant dining than a sandwich, can be found by continuing on Highway 89 to its junction with Highway 299. Five miles west is the town of Burney (pop. 3200) and 10 miles east is Fall River Mills (pop. 1500), both offering tourist amenities. Although I have camped within the park and, also, in one of the numerous forest service campgrounds dotting Highway 89 south, on another visit I will treat myself to an overnight in the Pit River Lodge. Built in 1921, the original structures housed workers who built the nearby power house known as "Pit One." The lodge now features a fine Craftsman-style central building and cabins along the river (details in the appendix).

If you traveled along the Trinity River Scenic Byway in Part One of this guide, you drove a portion of Highway 299, which dips like a lazy V across the width of California. From the Sacramento River, the highway rather closely follows the eastern route of the California to Oregon trail. In 1857, George Crook established a military fort on Fall River, a bit north of its confluence with the Pit River, to provide protection for those who wanted to settle in the valley, after the natives disputed the interlopers' right of passage.

Yes, he is the same George Crook who was at Fort Jones in Scott Valley in 1853, who led his troops south along the Military Pass Road, and who fought in the Civil War, to be awarded the rank of General. He was also involved in the capture of the Apache chief, Geronimo, in Mexico in 1886. Fort Crook no longer remains, but a museum in Fall River Mills keeps the history of the valley, and the story of the General, alive. It is open from May through October, Tuesday through Sunday.

Seventeen miles south of the junction of Highways 299 and 89, I turned onto Black Angus Lane to investigate Rancheria RV Park. It is what I term *a full service resort*, with roads leading around a fishing lake and level, grassy, pine-shaded hook-up sites, a general store, restaurant, and game room. Despite the appeal of the park, I decided to try it out on another trip and opted instead for one of the great forest service campgrounds along Hat Creek.

The last 22 miles of the Shasta Volcanic Scenic Byway along Highway 89 is a lovely run through rich ranch lands dotted with buttes on all sides. Tucked under a high lava escarpment on the east, the valley is watered by Hat

Creek, which flows quietly beside the road. Several forest service day-use picnic areas are located along the creek banks, all with nature trails and paths for fishermen. On the west, access roads lead to trailheads for the Thousand Lakes Wilderness, 16,000 acres of protected ponds and meadows, cinder cones, and lava tunnels. Permits can be obtained at the Hat Creek Ranger Station.

At the junction where north-south flowing Highway 89 meets east-west Highway 44, Lassen Volcanic Scenic Byway begins, and I hope you will continue to travel along with me.

134 « SCENIC BYWAYS

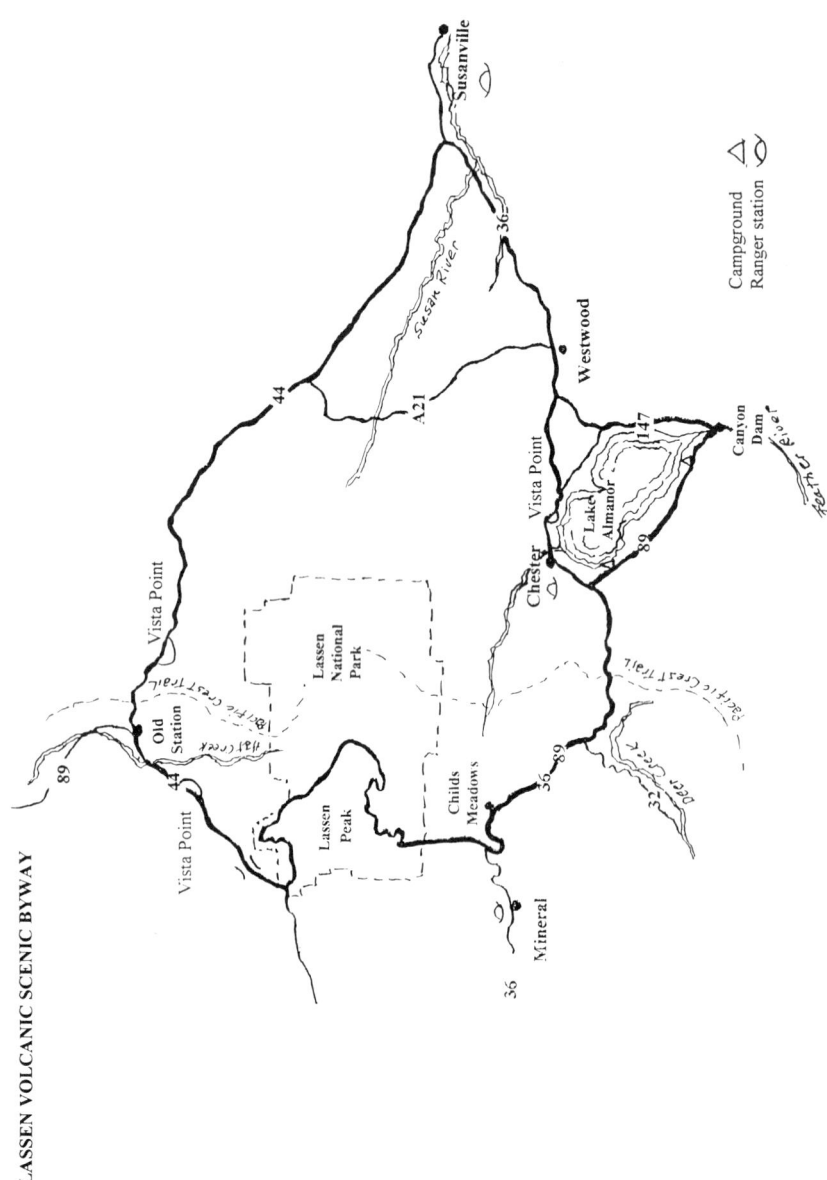

LASSEN VOLCANIC SCENIC BYWAY

Chapter X
LASSEN VOLCANIC SCENIC BYWAY
California State Highways 89, 44, 36 and 147
170 Miles

This byway does more than take you into the heart of Lassen Volcanic National Park. It leads you around the periphery to show you differing views of the buttes and craters that encircle Lassen Peak, like worshipers paying homage to a deity. This southernmost volcanic mountain in the Cascade Range is quite unlike Lava Beds or the Mt. Shasta region. To me it seemed like Yellowstone National Park in miniature.

As you journey south on Highway 89, it might be advisable to get fuel in Old Station at the junction of highways 89 and 44. The two routes run together for 13 miles, climbing to a scenic turnout on the left (about six miles from Old Station). I do suggest you pull in, park, and follow the upslope path (which has been cleared of scrubby chaparral) to see Lassen Peak, sparkling on the horizon. As with other rest stops, this one also provides comfort stations, picnic tables, and nature trails. Another seven miles takes you over Eskimo Hill Summit and down to the point where 44 continues west, and 89 branches off and leads through the national park. Immediately on the left, turn into Lassen Crossroads Information Center.

As a zealous devotee of interpretive centers, I can unequivocally declare this one rates five stars. Not only does it have the necessary facilities, and a parking area large enough for campers and big rigs, it offers a bonus. To see what I mean, follow the trail leading around huge exhibit boards sheltered by peaked roofs, a joint project of Lassen National Forest, the National Park Service, and Lassen Park Foundation. It was in the first stages of construction when I drove in. A national forest interpretive specialist later informed me that "the center is still evolving, with more exhibits due in the summer of 2002." The title "crossroads" refers to the center's location "where, the volcanoes of the Cascade Range, the granites of the Sierra Nevada, and the lava flows and faulting of the Great Basin meet." At the time of my visit, the displays were divided into four travel regions: A. Hat Creek Valley, B. Lassen Peak and Ishi Country, C. Lake Almanor, and D. Eagle Lake. The geology, plant and animal life, and human history of each region are described in narrative and photographs. Frankly, I can't wait to go back to see what has been added.

Because of deep snows, and the possibility of avalanches along the 30-mile parkway, this national park is only open from late spring to early fall. Just beyond the entrance station, you get your first view of Manzanita Lake, a panorama of forested shoreline with a backdrop of mountain peaks. The next curve in the road reveals Reflection Lake, an inverted image of Chaos Jumbles, a landslide of jagged boulders broken off from the top of Chaos Crags—tumbled down like a child's structure of building blocks. You will see chunks of the crinkled, pink lava put to good use in the walls and buildings of the Loomis Museum, named after the man who documented and photographed the peak's eruptions. His wonderful collection is displayed in the exhibit room of the museum across from Reflection Lake.

Before the 1980 eruption of Mount Saint Helens in Washington, Lassen Peak had been the most recent volcano in the Cascades to blow its top. In 1915, a mushroom cloud of fire and flame, smoke and ash, destroyed the terrain for miles around its base. In its wake, it left mounds and pinnacles of lava, rippling red dunes and deeply cut craters, boiling springs, and bubbling mudpots. But it also left alpine lakes and waterfalls, wildflower-studded meadows, and new-growth forests of pine and fir. You can view some of these wonders from the easy one-mile Lily Pond Nature Trail that begins at the museum or from the slightly longer Manzanita Lake Trail along the shore.

Across from the museum and built of the same pink stone is a small structure that houses a seismograph. Windows on each side give tourists a chance to observe the instrument that records earthquakes. The device is composed of a magnetic pendulum suspended between the poles of an electromagnet, which measures the land's motion and build-up of stress in the earth's surface. During a quake, a pen makes a heavy sweep of lines across the cylinder, recording the vibrations.

Beyond the museum and ranger station, a road leads south to the Manzanita Lake Campground, a series of

loops winding through the woods. During my first visit to the park, I lucked out in the smallest and last circle, finding shelter among the pines with a view of Lassen Peak outside my dinette window. Even if you aren't a camping person, drive the loops to see how the other half of the traveling population lives. It's a great way to go.

Past the campground road, the parkway swerves north and bends like a crimped horseshoe, twice crossing the Nobles Emigrant Trail. In 1852, several years after the major rush for gold had simmered down, William Nobles led a group of pioneers across the Great Basin, and veered off the Applegate Trail to head more directly west to the Sacramento River Valley. I can't help but wonder if any of those settlers came back after Lassen Peak's eruption to witness the pristine wilderness they had traveled through reduced to a scalded nothingness.

As you travel south again below Chaos Crags, you will pass the roadside exhibit of Hot Rock, explaining its displacement from the peaks above. Your next stop should be in the parking lot of the Devastated Area, nine miles from the entrance station. From this viewpoint you can clearly see Crescent Crater and Lassen Peak, with its V-shaped gullies created by lava flows. A half-mile, handicapped-accessible interpretive trail explains the earth's remarkable recovery from the eruptions. Although the disturbed area has been replanted with young conifers, the lack of a thick undergrowth of shrubs leaves the slopes looking barren and denuded.

Six miles farther, two campgrounds huddle beside Summit Lake, with a trail along the shoreline and a distant view of a series of lakes in deep basins to the east. The next point of interest is the Kings Creek picnic grounds and a three-mile round-trip trail to Kings Creek Falls—a serious photo-opportunity stop. The park road reaches its summit (elev. 8512 ft.) 22 miles from the entrance station, with Lassen Peak looming above. If you are inclined to hike the trail that leaves from here to the top of Lassen Peak, it's an uphill pull of 2000 feet, five miles round-trip.

On the mid-June day that I last drove around Lassen, the huge parking area was surrounded by six-foot snowbanks, and was almost completely filled with cars, motor homes, and pickups. I stopped for an in-camper cup of tea and watched stragglers begin their hike up and stragglers end their hike down. As I eavesdropped on their comments, I gathered the 100-mile view from the top was spectacular, as were the winds that nearly swept them off the peak.

Descending the shoulder of the summit, two glass-smooth, blue-green lakes reflect the rocky crags behind. Between them, the Bumpass Hell trail takes off—a three-mile round-trip hike through the hot springs area. After a 500-foot climb, the trail descends into the largest thermal area in the park, leading around and over volcanic vents. A boardwalk with a railing protects the public from crashing through the crust, as did the first white man to hike in this awesome place.

From the nature-trail pamphlet and the signposts along the way, I learned that the site was named for the man who discovered it in 1865, Kendall Vanhook Bumpass. He lost a leg from burns he suffered when he stepped into a boiling mudpot. As I leaned on the railing and looked down, I could visualize mother earth seething far below the surface, ready to blow at any time: a fourteenth century Dante's inferno and a twentieth century surrealist painting by Salvador Dali.

If you don't take this walk, you will have another chance to get close to the powder keg that lies under these mountain ranges. After winding down the south flank of Lassen Peak for three miles, a sign directs you to the parking area for the Sulphur Works. Again, a boardwalk leads around the stinking vents, remnants of Lassen Peak's ghostly ancestor, ancient Mt. Tehama. Signposts along the way tell you the story.

Like picture postcards of pristine, sun-filled scenes, my days in this park were just that, but I would like to witness the thunder god Thor rip and rumble, bunch up pewter-gray clouds over the peaks, and let her rip. Not, however, when I'm on the trail, but snug and safe in my camper, watching *The Tempest* enacted on the grandest of all stages.

If at this point you need more information about the geological wonders you've experienced during your drive, pull into one of the large parking loops that surround the Southwest Information Station, just a mile down the road. You can also treat yourself to whatever will revive your energy at the Lassen Chalet. A hot fudge sundae and cup of coffee certainly helped to restore mine and gave me the impetus to look for overnight lodging. Although a forest service campground is tucked into the woods beyond the parking lot, I wanted more amenities that night than boondocking offered.

Since this scenic byway touches four counties, you might think there would be numerous choices for lodging. Our route begins in Shasta County, crosses a snippet of Tehama, proceeds along an upper section of Plumas, and returns north through the southwestern part of Lassen County. However, the highways are almost completely enveloped by national forests and wilderness areas, with a scarcity of towns.

As you leave the park, one option is to drive four miles west of the junction of highways 89 and 36 to Mineral, the location of Lassen National Park Headquarters. The Mineral Lodge has been welcoming travelers since 1880 and continues to provide a motel, restaurant, and a store. Volcano Country RV Park, under the same management, offers a full-service camping resort.

For the next 25 miles, highways 89 and 36 share joint custody of the scenic byway. We will continue east, ascend Morgan Summit, with its huge snowmobile parking lot, and descend to cross Mill Creek. The pastoral serenity of daisies leaning yellow heads against split-rail fences is a delightful contrast to the tumultuous terrain we recently traversed. On the left you will see Childs Meadow Resort, its sign hanging from log posts topped by four metal sculptures of deer. The long, low white building houses a cafe and general store. The campground and a group of cabins are dwarfed by a thick stand of towering conifers.

Nine miles past the resort, Highway 32 leads southwest for 56 winding, precipitous miles down into the Sacramento River Valley. The upper section of the road traces Peter Lassen's trail, until it veers off to follow Deer Creek down to his rancho, which was located on present-day Highway 99 between Chico and Red Bluff. We will come across another portion of what the emigrants called "Lassen's Death Route" a bit farther along the byway that bears his name.

About a mile beyond the Highway 32 turn-off, another option for an overnight stay and sustenance appears on the right. The St. Bernard Lodge, an historic inn dating from 1929, provides a knotty-pine dining room and tavern in the lower level, with guest rooms on the second floor. The owners also offer camping sites under the pines or in the meadow behind.

A mile beyond the lodge, the Pacific Crest Trail crosses the highway and, after another eight miles, Highway 89 veers south around Lake Almanor. But now, we will forge ahead on Highway 36 to the little town of Chester. The road widens to become Main Street, with the forest service ranger district station on the left and Plumas County Airport on the right. Watch for the Chamber of Commerce at 529 Main Street, also on the right, and ask for the current issue of the *Plumas County Visitors' Guide*. You might also inquire about dining and lodging facilities, but many tourists think The Bidwell House Bed and Breakfast Inn at #1 Main Street is the "in place."

Whatever you decide about overnight accommodations, the powers that be decided that the Lassen Volcanic Scenic Byway should pass south of Highway 36, track Highway 89 around Lake Almanor's western side, turn abruptly north on Highway 147 on the lake's eastern side and then rejoin Highway 36. Complicated? Yes, but if you look at the map you will note this odd, tacked-on, turtle-tail configuration. However, it is a pleasant drive and we will do as directed.

Created in 1914 by damming the North Fork of the Feather River to provide hydroelectric power, Lake Almanor's name originated by taking letters from the names of the company vice president's three daughters: Alice, Martha and Elinore. As the waters of the reservoir inundated farms, ranches, and resorts in Big Meadows, the village of Prattville and an Indian cemetery were moved to higher ground.

When the original company became part of Pacific Gas and Electric, the lake was developed as a recreational area in conjunction with the Lassen National Forest Service. Under the auspices of both, there are campgrounds, picnic areas, beaches, and boat ramps around the western shore. A nine-mile, paved, barrier-free trail, offering scenic vistas and interpretive sites, takes off from the Lake Almanor PG&E Campground at the southern end of the lake. On numerous occasions, I have parked my camper on one of the sites beside the beach, watched the setting sun cast rippled shadows on the water, and been awakened by its rays topping the eastern hills.

This western side of the lake is deeply wooded, with limited lake views from the highway, unless you take one of the side roads leading to the shore. After crossing the causeway over the Feather River outlet, you arrive at Canyon Dam, which has a general store and several private RV parks. Make an abrupt left turn onto Highway 147 and proceed north on the lake's eastern side. After a quarter-mile drive, a turnout on the left side offers a splendid view of Lake Almanor, with Lassen Peak hazy in the distance. After another quarter-mile, watch for a downhill loop to an oak-shaded picnic area.

The southern portion of Highway 147 carries heavy traffic, with private homes and resorts on both sides of the road. After about eight miles, you have the option of veering northeast on Highway 147 for another three miles to Highway 36, or turning left on Peninsula Road, which also leads to Highway 36 and back to Chester. There are a couple good reasons for returning to Chester: a vista point high on the hill offers an expansive overview of the lake and, at the foot of the hill, the drive across a long bridge into town offers a water's edge view up the northern arm of the lake.

Whatever your decision, in order to complete the Lassen Volcanic Scenic Byway loop, you need to follow Highway 36 east for 30 miles and turn north on Highway 44. Along the way, you will pass the historic lumber town of Westwood, celebrated not only for supporting the largest sawmill in the West, but for its 25-foot statue of the legendary logger, Paul Bunyan. A mythical transplant from Minnesota?

After crossing the Union Pacific Railroad tracks, an important part of this timber country's history, you can make a quick drive through the quaint village by turning south on Mooney Road. Look for the statue next to the museum, and perhaps have lunch in Buffalo Chip's Pizza Cafe, housed in an historic bunkhouse.

On the other side of Highway 36, Mooney Road (A21) again traces the Lassen Trail, along which Peter Lassen led his weary emigrants south. If you will remember from my brief discussion in Chapter VII, he had returned to Missouri in 1847, hoping to encourage a group of pioneers to settle around his rancho. Alas, heading north from the Humboldt River in Nevada, he went too far north, crossed the Fandango Pass into northeastern California, followed the Pit River for awhile, veered east of the volcanic peak that would bear his name, went west through Big Meadows, and came along the ridge between Mill Creek and Deer Creek down to the Sacramento River. It's no wonder later emigrants avoided Lassen's treacherous trail.

We continue east on Highway 36, curve up to top Fredonyer Pass and drop down to the junction of Highway 44, clearly marked with scenic byway signs, and the route we will be taking—after a slight detour. You have now left Plumas County and crossed into Lassen County, an area that stretches east across the Honey Lake Valley to Nevada and north to the Modoc County line.

The first white settler in the valley, Isaac Roop, built a trading post on the Nobles Emigrant Trail in 1852, a trail that did not wander all the way north as Lassen's did but forged almost due west from the Humboldt River. After Lassen sold his ranch on Deer Creek in 1850, and joined other treasure hunters in the Sierra Mountains, he discovered gold around Honey Lake. This strike encouraged an influx of miners. According to legend, Roop, Lassen, and a group of these early settlers named the area the Territory of Nataqua in 1856, not knowing whether they were in California or were a part of Utah Territory. These bits of history (including the meaning of Nataqua) you will learn if you visit Susanville, the seat of government for Lassen County. It's only five miles beyond the Highway 44 turn-off, and the detour will be time well spent. Highway 36 curves downhill to Main Street, and on the corner of Lassen Street you will immediately note a wall-size mural of Isaac Roop and his daughter, Susan for whom the town was named.

This is a town of many murals. To obtain a visitors' guide and a map, turn left on North Lassen and drive one block to the Chamber of Commerce on the corner of Nevada Street. Be sure to get directions to Roop's Fort in Memorial Park on Weatherow, one-half block off Main Street. Built in 1854, the log cabin was known as Roop's House, and became a welcome way station for travelers on the Nobles Em-

igrant Trail. The volunteers in the museum next door will be happy to tell the tale of the "Sagebrush War," a brief battle between the good folks of the short-lived Nataqua Territory and the sheriff of Plumas County.

After you have strolled the downtown streets to see the eight large murals, drive east on Main past the Lassen County Fairgrounds, and turn right on Riverside Drive. The Bureau of Land Management and Lassen National

Forest Headquarters are both on the south side—if you are looking for information about camping and hiking trails in the back country. Continue across the Susan River to Richmond, and turn left to visit the historic Susanville train depot, adjacent to the Southern Pacific Railroad tracks.

The depot serves as trailhead for Lassen County's most celebrated attraction—the Bizz Johnson Trail. The trail follows a branch-line railroad track built in 1914 to provide a link between the logging communities of Lassen County and the railroad's main line in Nevada. Used by hikers, joggers, horseback riders, and bicyclists, it winds for 25 miles along the West Fork of the Susan River, crosses 11 bridges, and goes through two tunnels. The rail trail pamphlet, complete with a detailed map and illustrations, makes for interesting reading.

If you wish to complete the Lassen Volcanic Scenic Byway loop, you will need to backtrack to Highway 44, and drive 46 miles northwest to the junction with Highway 89 at Old Station. There are no towns along the way but the route through Lassen National Forest is lovely. You will be traveling around ranch lands watered by reservoirs, and the Susan River winds placidly south from its headwaters in the Caribou Wilderness. Side roads lead off to prime fishing spots: Feather Lake and Crater Lake.

As the highway rises to traverse a high plateau, watch for the very large parking area of the Bogard Visitor Information Center on the left. At the risk of overusing superlatives, the vistas in all directions are dazzling. To the north, Hat Creek Valley and the merest white tip of Mount Shasta are visible, while directly below and to the west, the domes and cinder cones, the buttes and lakes surrounding Lassen Peak come into view.

After a short trail-walk along the bluff, I sat on a stone wall and contemplated the rugged country spread before me like a topographical map. Legend says that Jedediah Smith came this way and, if I could but see beyond the mountains down into the Sacramento River Valley, I would be able to pick up his footprints along the Trinity River— where this odyssey around the Siskiyous, the Klamaths, the Trinity Alps, and the Cascades began.

BIBLIOGRAPHY

Arnold, Mary Elliott and Mabel Reed. *In the Land of the Grasshopper Song.* Lincoln: University of Nebraska Press, 1980 reprint. A delightful story of two New Jersey women, employed by the U.S. Indian Service as Field Matrons in the Klamath River Indian country in 1908-1909.

Bell, Maureen. *Karuk: The Upriver People.* Happy Camp, CA: Naturegraph Publishers, 1991. An "easy to read" little book about the Karuks, written by an anthropologist who had friends in the tribe.

Bennion, Ben & Jerry Rohde. *Traveling the Trinity Highway.* McKinleyville, CA: Mountain Home Books, 2000. Excellent historical research conducted by professors and students of Humboldt State University. Illustrated with photographs.

Brewer, William. *Up and Down California in 1860-1864.* Berkeley, CA: University of California Press, 1949-1966, 3rd. Edition. Reprints of articles appearing in Harper's Monthly & Century Magazine.

Carson, Rachel. *Silent Spring.* Boston, MA: Houghton Miflin, 1962.

Cline, Gloria Griffin. *Peter Skene Ogden and the Hudson's Bay Company.* Norman, OK: University of Oklahoma Press, 1974. A well researched biography with an extensive bibliography.

Forbes, Jack. *Native Americans of California and Nevada.* Happy Camp, CA: Naturegraph Publishers, 1982, reprinted 1991. Deals primarily with the historical and cultural experiences which have contributed to the present-day condition of western American Indians.

Fremont, John Charles. *Narratives of Exploration and Adventure; 1843-1846*, edited by Allan Nevins. New York: Longmans, Green & Co., 1956. Written with colorful descriptions of the country traveled by Fremont and his men.

Gordon, David George. *Field Guide to the Sasquatch.* Seattle: Sasquatch Books, 1992. A slim volume of 47 pages suggesting the reader "Follow in the footsteps of North America's most elusive animal." With maps of Bigfoot territory.

Green, David & Greg Ingold. *Marble Mountain Wilderness.* Berkeley: Wilderness Press, 1996. Good descriptions of geology, botany and zoology as well as details of 28 hikes. Includes a topographical map.

Green, John. *Sasquatch: The Apes Among Us.* Blaine, WA: Hancock House Publishers, 1978. A complete 480 page history of Bigfoot sightings and research in British Columbia, California, Washington, Oregon, Montana, and Idaho.

Gudde, Erwin G. *California Gold Camps.* Berkeley: University of California Press, 1975. Short descriptions of each mining camp. Begun in 1960 as an outgrowth of Gudde's *California Place Names* (1948) completed before his death in 1969 but not published until 1975 by his wife, Elizabeth.

Harris, Stephen L. *Agents of Chaos.* Missoula, MT: Mountain Press Publishing Company, 1990. A helpful book in understanding the rumblings of the earth.

_____. *Fire Mountains of the West.* Missoula: Mountain Press Publishing Co., 1998 revision of *Fire and Ice,* 1976. Complete descriptions of the volcano peaks of the Cascade Range.

Hart, John. *Hiking the Bigfoot Country: The Wildlands of Northern California and Southern Oregon.* Sierra Club Tote Book, 1975. A good take-along book for hikers.

Heizer, Robert F. and Albert B. Elsasser. *The Natural World of the California Indians.* Berkeley: University of California Press, 1980.

Hoeper, George. *Black Bart: Boulevardier Bandit.* Fresno, CA: Word Dancer Press, 1995. A history of Wells Fargo Express Company, the detective who trailed Charles Bolton (Black Bart) and a biography of the "gentleman bandit."

Hoover, Mildred Brooke & H.E. & E.G. Rensch. *Historic Spots in California.* Third Edition, revised by William N. Abeloe. Stanford: Stanford University Press, 1966. A first rate, 640 page book originally published in three volumes from 1932 to 1937, condensed into one volume covering each county in California.

Hyndam, Donald & David Alt. *Roadside Geology of Northern and Central California.* Missoula, MT: Mountain Press, 1999. An excellent book for anyone seriously interested in the complex but intriguing geology of the Klamath and Trinity Alps, the Cascades and Sierra Nevada Mountains.

Kelly, David. *Secrets of the Old Growth Forest.* Layton, UT: Gibbs Smith Publishers, 1988.

Kittredge, William. *Hole in the Sky: A Memoir.* New York: Alfred A. Knopf, 1992.

Knudtson, Peter M. *The Wintun Indians of California and Their Neighbors.* Happy Camp, CA: Naturegraph Publishers, 1977. Provides a great deal of information about the Wintun, Shasta, Karuk and Yurok Indians.

Kroeber, A.L. *Handbook of the Indians of California.* Bureau of American Ethnology, Smithsonian Institution, Bulletin #78, 1925. New York: Dover Publications, Reprint, 1976. The original and ultimate authority on the natives of California.

Linkhart, Luther & Michael White. *The Trinity Alps: A Hiking and Backpacking Guide.* Berkeley, CA: Wilderness Press, 1994. Includes natural history, geology, climate, plants and animals. Describes 32 trips over 500 miles of trails, detailing highway access.

Morgan, Dale L. *Jedediah Smith and the Opening of the West.* Lincoln: University of Nebraska Press, 1953. A comprehensive history of the American and Canadian fur trapping companies, with biographies of other mountain men besides Jedediah Smith.

Moss, Wayne F. *The Trinity Alps Companion: Hiking Trails and Angling Tales in the California Wilderness.* Ecopress, Chris Beatty, publisher, 1997. Reviews by hikers are terrific.

Nadeau, Remi. *Ghost Towns & Mining Camps of California: a History & Guide.* Santa Barbara, CA: Crest Publishers, 1965-1992. Another easy-to-read book for anyone interested in the subject. Includes clear, concise maps.

Nunes, Dr. Doyce B. Jr. *The Bidwell-Bartleson Party, 1841: California Emigrants and Adventurers, the Documents and Memoirs of the Overland Pioneers.* Santa Cruz, CA: Western Tanager Press, 1991. An excellent book which includes journal accounts, narratives by other members of the party, extracts from letters and biographical sketches of the overland pioneers.

Ogden, Peter Skeene. *Traits of American Indian Life and Character.* New York: Dover Publications, 1995. An interesting and insightful account written by "A Fur Trader" and attributed to Peter Ogden.

Palmer, Tim. *The Wild and Scenic Rivers of America.* Washington, DC and Covelo, CA: Island Press, 1993. An excellent book giving a lot of details about the designation of wild and scenic rivers, and those already approved by 1993.

Powers, Stephen. *Tribes of California, Vol. III of Contributions to North American Ethnology.* Washington, DC: Department of the Interior, Government Printing Office, 1877. Reprint, University of California Press, Berkeley, CA, 1977.

Rawls, James J. *Indians of California: The Changing Image.* Norman, OK: University of Oklahoma Press, 1984.

Riddle, Jeff C. *The Indian History of the Modoc War.* Eugene, OR: Urion Press, 1974. Reprint of 1914 account. Written by an uneducated Modoc, whose father was involved in the war. It is slow reading but completely detailed, with biographies of other participants.

Roberts, George & Jan. *Discover Historic California*. Whittier, CA: New Fortress Publications, 1986. Divided into 76 regions with brief descriptions of historic sites.

Schaffer, Jeffery P. *The Pacific Crest Trail, Vol. 1, California*. Berkeley: Wilderness Press, 1981. A personal narrative of hiking the trail with interesting anecdotes.

_____, *Lassen Volcanic National Park and Vicinity: A Natural History Guide*. Berkeley: Wilderness Press, 1986.

Selters, Andy & Michael Zanger. *The Mt. Shasta Book*. Berkeley: Wilderness Press, 2001.

Soares, John R. & Marc J. *100 Classic Hikes in Northern California*. Seattle, WA: The Mountaineers, 2000. Good directions and maps to Trinity Alps, Cascades, Lassen and Northern Sierra Nevada.

_____. *75 Hikes in California's Lassen Park and Mount Shasta Regions*. Seattle: The Mountaineers, 1996.

Stienstra, Tom. *Foghorn Outdoors: California Camping: The Complete Guide*. Avalon Travel Publications, 12th edition, 2001. This book is truly a "complete guide" to more than 1500 campgrounds. A 776 page "take-along" for tent campers, van campers, and RVers.

Steinberg, Sabra L., Jeffery R. Dunk & Tall Chief A. Comet. *In Hoopa Territory*. Office of Research & Development, PO Box 1348, Hoopa, CA 95546, 2000. A guide to back roads and trails on the Hoopa Reservation, with excellent details about the flora and fauna encountered.

Sullivan, Maurice S. *The Travels of Jedediah Smith: A Documentary Outline Including the Journal of the Great American Pathfinder*. Santa Ana, CA: The Fine Arts Press, 1934. An historical treasure of the pathfinder's journal notations.

Wallace, David Rains. *The Klamath Knot*. Covelo, CA: Yolla Bolly Press, Sierra Club, 1983. Although this book concerns the natural world of the Klamath Mountains, this is not a dry scientific treatise! It is lyrical, readable and understandable, full of mythology and psychic awareness of nature.

SOURCES OF INFORMATION

NOTE: This valuable section of the book for planning your trips ahead, or useful when on the road, is up-to-date at press time. However addresses and phone numbers do change. For the accuracy of future editions, we'd appreciate your help by calling 1-800 390-5353 or e-mail nature@sisqtel.net if you discover changes. Thank you, Naturegraph.

PART ONE: NORTHWESTERN CALIFORNIA

California Department of Boating & Waterways, 2000 Evergreen Street, Suite 100, Sacramento, CA 95815-3888 • (916) 263-4326 • (888) 326-2822   www.dbw.ca.gov

California Department of Fish & Game, 1416 Ninth Street, Sacramento, CA 95814 •(916) 445-0411   www.dfg.ca.gov

California Department of Parks & Recreation, P.O. Box 942896, Sacramento, CA 94296 • (916) 653-6995 • (800) 777-0369 www.parks.ca.gov   info@parks.ca.gov

California Department of Transportation, P.O. Box 942873, Sacramento, CA 94273 • (916) 654-5286 • (800) 427-7623 www.dot.ca.gov/hq/roadinfo Enter Highway #.

Klamath National Forest, 1312 Fairlane Road, Yreka, CA 96097 • (530) 842-6131   www.r5.fs.fed.us/klamath

Pacific Crest Trail Association, 5325 Elkhorn Blvd. #256, Sacramento, CA 95842 •(916) 349-2109   www.pcta.org   e-mail: info@pcta.org.

Shasta-Trinity National Forest, 2400 Washington Ave., Redding, CA 96001 • (530) 244-2978   www.r5.fs.fed.us/shastatrinity

Siskiyou National Forest, P.O. Box 440, Grants Pass, OR, 97526 • (541) 471-6500   www.r5.fs.fed.us/siskiyou

Six Rivers National Forest, 1330 Bayshore Way, Eureka, CA 95501, • (707) 442-1721   www.r5.fs.fed.us/sixrivers

Do check the webpages of the national forests listed above. They contain a wealth of information about all the recreational possibilities within the forests and wilderness areas, with addresses for district ranger stations, maps, and photos.

Websites of interest and information:

National Wildlife Federation,   www.nwf.org

Native American Heritage Commission,   www.nahc.ca.gov

Wilderness Society,   www.wilderness.net

On-line Forest Service Magazine,   www.ournationalforests.com

SMITH RIVER SCENIC BYWAY

Crescent City-Del Norte County Chamber of Commerce, 1001 Front Street, Crescent City, CA 95531 • (707) 464-3174 • (800) 343-8300 www.northerncalifornia.net

Jedediah Smith Redwoods State Park, Highway 199, Hiouchi, CA 95531 • (707) 464-6101 Visitor center; beach picnic area, tables and BBQs; 106 campsites, table, fire ring, water, restrooms, hot showers, sanitation station, no hookups. Open all year. www.parks.ca.gov

Redwood National & State Parks Headquarters, 1111 Second Street, Crescent City, CA 95531 • (707) 464-6101 Hiouchi Information Center, Highway 199, open 9-5 summer only. www.nps.gov/redw

Save the Redwoods League, 114 Sansome Street, Room 605, San Francisco, CA, 94104 • (415) 362-2352 www.savetheredwoods.org

Smith River National Recreation Area, 10600 Highway 199, P.O. Box 228, Gasquet, CA 95543 • (707) 457-3131 www.delnorte.org/smra

Dining and Lodging

Hiouchi Cafe & Motel, 2095 Highway 199, Hiouchi, CA 95531 • (888) 881-0819 www.tiki.net/~jkistler email: diving@tiki.net

Patrick Creek Lodge, 13950 Highway 199, Gasquet, CA 95543 Bill and Cindy Grier, owners. (707) 457-3323 www.patrickcreeklodge.com

TRINITY RIVER SCENIC BYWAY

Blue Lake Chamber of Commerce, P.O. Box 476, Blue Lake, CA 95525 • (707) 668-5180

Hayes Bookstore, 106 Main Street, Weaverville, CA 96093 • (530) 623-2516

Highland Art Center, 503 Main Street, Weaverville, CA 96093 • (530) 623-5111 Open May-December 10-5 Monday-Saturday, 11-4 Sunday. January through April closed Sundays.

Shasta State Historic Park, P.O. Box 2430, Shasta, CA 90687 • (530) 243-8194 Museum open 10-5 Wednesday-Sunday, closed Thanksgiving, Christmas & New Year's Day. www.parks.ca.gov/shastacascade

Trinity County Arts Council, P.O. Box 1887, Weaverville, CA 96093 • (530) 623-2760 www.tcarts.com

Trinity County Chamber of Commerce, P.O. Box 517, Weaverville, CA 96093 • 211 Trinity Lakes Blvd. (Highway 3) • (530) 623-6101 • (800) 487-4648 www.trinitycounty.com email: chamber@trinitycounty.com

Trinity County Historical Society, P.O. Box 333, 508 Main Street, Weaverville, CA 96093 • (530) 623-5211 Jackson Memorial Museum, open daily May 1 to October 31, 10-5. www.tcoe.trinity.k12.ca.us/~museum

Trinity Journal, P.O. Box 340, 218 Main Street, Weaverville, CA 96093 • (530) 623-2055

Trinity National Forest, Weaverville Ranger Station, P.O. Box 1190, Weaverville, CA 96093 • (530) 623-2121

Trinity River Rafting, P.O. Box 572, Big Bar, CA 96010 • (530) 623-3033 • (800) 307-4837   www.trinitycountyrafting.com

Weaverville Joss House, Main and Oregon Streets, Weaverville, CA 96093 • (530) 623-5284. Guided tours daily in summer, Wednesday-Sunday spring-fall, Sundays in winter. Modest fee.

Whiskeytown National Recreation Area, P.O. Box 188, Whiskeytown, CA 96095. Park Headquarters (530) 241-6584, Visitor Center (530) 246-1225. Open daily Memorial Day through Labor Day. www.nps.gov/whis

Dining and Lodging

La Grange Cafe, 216 Main Street, Weaverville, CA 96093 • (530) 623-5325

Numerous motels in Weaverville from AAA three-star rated **Victorian Inn** (530) 623-4432 to the two-star rated **49er Gold County Inn** (530) 623-4937 www.49ermotel.com. The **Red Hill Motel**, Willie and Patty Holder, owner/operators, (530) 623-4331 is reminiscent of motor-courts of the 1940s. www.redhillresorts.com

Because I travel like a turtle with my own shelter, my lodging site is provided by an RV Park, designed and constructed by RVer owner-managers, retired Trinity County Superintendent of Schools, Don Stewart and his wife Clara. The reception building, terraced sites, clean restrooms, and laundry facilities, and friendly welcome, all make this highly recommended. (See listing below.)

Sidney Gulch RV Park, Highway 299 & Tinnen St., Weaverville, CA 96093 • (530) 623-6621 • (800) 554-1626   www.c-zone.net/sgrvpark
e-mail: sgrvpark@c-zone.net

French Gulch Hotel, P.O. Box 310, 14138 Main Street, French Gulch, CA 96033 • (530) 359-2112. Owner/chef Andrew Bouchard & wife Carol Jandrall. An historic inn, open March through December, B&B with 8 rooms. Restaurant open Thursday through Saturday 5-9, Sunday brunch 9-1. www.frenchgulchhotel.com   email: rangercec@aol.com

Accommodations along the remainder of Highway 299 are sparse, limited to cabins and cottages in several RV campgrounds. Check with the Trinity County Chamber of Commerce for recommendations.

BIGFOOT SCENIC BYWAY

Bigfoot Field Research Organization: A data-base by region, recent reports and articles. www.bfro.net.

Big Foot Golf & Country Club, P.O. Box 836, Willow Creek, CA 95573. Pro-shop: (530) 629-2977 • (800) 788-9548, Dining Room: (530) 629-2193

Hoopa Tribal Museum, P.O. Box 1348, Hoopa, CA 95546 • (530) 625-4110. Open Monday through Friday, 8-5, closed 12-1.

Hoopa Tribal Office, P.O. Box 817, Hoopa, CA 95546 • (530) 625-4211

152 « SCENIC BYWAYS

Lower Trinity Ranger District, Highway 96, P.O. Box 68, Willow Creek, CA 95573 • (530) 629-2118

Orleans Chamber of Commerce, Highway 96, P.O. Box 211, Orleans, CA 95556 • (530) 627-3454 Open 8-12, week days.

Orleans Ranger District, Ishi Pishi Road, P.O Box 410, Orleans, CA 95556 • (530) 627-3291

The Scientific Study of Hidden Animals: includes all strange, rare and mythical creatures, including Sasquatch. www.cryptozoology.com

Wild By Nature Environmental Center, Orleans, CA 95556. Dr. Kathryn Wild, Director, 7275 Canyon Breeze, San Diego, CA 92126 •(858) 271-8280 www.wildbynature.org   e-mail: info@wildbynature.org

Willow Creek Chamber of Commerce, P.O. Box 704, Willow Creek, CA 95573 (530) 629-2693   www.willowcreekchamber.com
e-mail: info@willowcreekchamber.com

Willow Creek-China Flat Museum, P.O. Box 102, Willow Creek, CA 95573 • (530) 629-2653 Open Friday, Saturday, Sunday 10-4, May through September

Dining and Lodging

Cinnabar Sam's, 19 Willow Way & Highway 299, Willow Creek, CA 95573 • (530) 629-3437. Reasonable prices, great quality and quantity. Friendly owners and staff. Recommended.

Big Foot Motel, City Center, P.O. Box 957, Willow Creek, CA 95573 (530) 629-2115 Two-story, clean and comfortable with pool. www.bigfootmotel.com

Klamath Riverside RV Park, Highway 96, P.O. Box 236, Orleans, CA 95556 • (530) 627-3239 •(800) 627-9779 Karen & Mark O'Rourke, owner/operators. Beautifully maintained, friendly owners who treat their campers like family. www.klamathriversidervpark.com
e-mail: Klamathrvpark@hotmail.com

Lazy Double "B" Campground & RV Park, P.O. Box 527, Salyer, CA 95563 •(530) 629-2156.   Highway 299, 5 miles east of Willow Creek.

Marble Mountain Ranch, 92520 Highway 96, Somes Bar, CA 95568 • (530) 469-3322 • (800) 552-6284. Doug & Heidi Cole, owners. This family owned and operated guest ranch, offers river running, horse back riding, and accommodations from small cabins to a spacious lodge. During the season (April through September) meals are served in a pleasant dining room. www.marblemountainranch.com

Otter Bar Lodge & Kayak School, Box 210, Forks of the Salmon, CA 96031 • (530) 462-4772. Located fifteen miles up the Salmon River Road, this is a wilderness lodge for 14 persons, offering a first-rate kayaking school, guided horseback trips into the Trinity Alps, fly-fishing clinics, and kids camps. www.otterbar.com   e-mail: otterbar@aol.com

Tsewenaldin Inn, P.O. Box 219, Hoopa, CA 95546 •(530) 625-4294. Highway 96, next to the Hoopa Center. A two-story motel over-looking the Trinity River.

STATE OF JEFFERSON SCENIC BYWAY

Eagles Nest Golf Club, 22112 Walker Rd. Klamath River, CA 96050 • (530) 465-2424 • (888) 782-5634

Happy Camp Chamber of Commerce, P.O. Box 1188, Happy Camp, CA 96039 • (530) 493-2900

Happy Camp Community Computer Center, Fourth Ave. & Washington, Happy Camp, CA 96039 • (530) 493-5213

Happy Camp Ranger District, Hwy. 96 & Park Way, P.O. Box 377, Happy Camp, CA 96039 • (530) 493-2243

Karuk Tribe of California, 64236 Second Ave. P.O. Box 1016, Happy Camp, CA 96039 • (530) 493-5305

Naturegraph Publishers, 3543 Indian Creek Rd., P.O. Box 1047, Happy Camp, CA 96039 •(530) 493-5353 • (800) 390-5353 www.naturegraph.com e-mail: nature@sisqtel.net

River Country Rafting, P.O. Box 319, Happy Camp, CA 96039 • (530) 493-2207. Joe & Becca Cote Giera, operators. Private party raft trips. www.klamathrafting.8k.com

The New 49ers, Inc, 27 Davis Rd. P.O. Box 47, Happy Camp, CA 96039 • (530) 493-2012   www.goldgold.com

The State of Jefferson Chamber, P.O. Box 521, Seiad Valley, CA 96086 • (530) 496-3325   www.Jeffersonstate.com

Websites of interest & information:

www.happycampnews.com An online newsletter

Dining and Lodging

Elk Creek Camp & RV Park, P.O. Box 318, Happy Camp, CA 96039 •(530) 493-2208. Owners, Eddie & Jean Davenport. Highly recommended. www.elkcreekcampground.com e-mail: eddiedav@sisqtel.net

Forest Lodge Motel, 63712 Highway 96, P.O. Box 1535, Happy Camp, CA 96039 • (530) 493-5296. Owners, Brinda & Gary Hulsey. www.forestlodgemotel.com

Frontier Cafe, 64118 Second Ave. & Highway 96, Happy Camp, CA 96039 • (530) 493-2242

Seiad Valley Store & Restaurant, 44719 Highway 96, Seiad Valley, CA 96086 • (530) 496-3399

Sportsman's Lodge, 20502 Highway 96, Klamath River, CA 96050 • (530) 465-2366

Thompson Creek Lodge, 52431 Highway 96, Seiad Valley, CA 96086 • (530) 496-3657 www.sisqtel.net/~cnelson

Wildwood, 45200 Highway 96, Seiad Valley, CA 96086 • (530) 496-3195

TRINITY HERITAGE SCENIC BYWAY

Alpen Cellars, Rt. 2, Box 3966, Trinity Center, CA 96091 • (530) 266-3363. Mark Groves, Manager, Keith Groves, Winemaker.

Coffee Creek Country Store, Highway 3 & Coffee Creek Road, Trinity Center, CA 96091 • (530) 266-3233

Coffee Creek Ranger Station, Trinity Center, CA 96091 • (530) 266-3211. Open summer only.

Etna Brewing Co., 131 Callahan Street, Etna, CA 96027 • (530) 467-5277. Open 5 pm for tours and tasting, closed Monday & Tuesday.

Fort Jones Museum, P.O. Box 428, 11913 Main Street, Fort Jones, CA 96032 • (530) 468-5568. Open summer, Monday through Saturday.

Scott Valley Alpacas, P.O. Box 58, 3135 North Kidder Creek Road, Greenview, CA 96037 • (530) 468-2819. John and Beth Franklin invite visitors, if you phone ahead. www.sisqtel.net/~alpaca e-mail: alpaca@sisqtel.net

Scott Valley Chamber of Commerce, P.O. Box 111, Greenview, CA 96037 • (530) 467-5153   http://come.to/scott-valley   jayackerman@yahoo.com

Scott River Ranger District, Klamath National Forest, 11263 No. Highway 3, Fort Jones, CA 96032-9702 • (530) 468-5351

Siskiyou County Museum, 910 Main Street, Yreka, CA 96097 • (530) 842-3836. Open 9-5, Tuesday through Saturday; admission $1 adults, .75 for children 7-12.

Siskiyou Daily News, P.O. Box 129, 309 S. Broadway, Yreka, CA 96097 • (530) 842-5777   www.siskiyoudaily.com

The Pioneer Press, P.O. Box 400, 12021 Main Street, Fort Jones, CA 96032 • (530) 468-5355

Yreka Chamber of Commerce, 117 W. Miner Street, Yreka, CA 96097 • (530) 842-1649   www.yrekachamber.com e-mail: a-yreka@inreach.com

Yreka Western Railroad, P.O. Box 660, 300 E. Miner Street, Yreka, CA 96097 •(530) 842-4146 •(800) 973-5277   www.yrekawesternrr.com

Dining and Lodging

Bob's Ranch House, 585 Collier Way, Etna, CA 96027 • (530) 467-5787. A local gathering place, friendly and pleasant spot for a bite to eat.

Bradley's Alderbrook Manor, 836 Main Street, Etna, CA 96027 • (530) 467-3917. Five guest rooms, back deck overlooking two acres of gardens. www.sisqtel.net/~joybrad e-mail: joybrad@sisqtel.net

Carrville Inn, Rt. 2, Box 3536, Trinity Center, CA 96091 • (530) 266-3511. Dave & Sheri Overly, owners. Historic inn, the ultimate in B&B luxury, beautiful setting. www.carrvilleinn.com e-mail: info@carrvilleinn.com

Coffee Creek Ranch, 4940 Coffee Creek Road, Trinity Center, CA 96091 • (530) 266-3343 •(800) 624-4480 www.coffeecreekranch.com

Grandma's House, 123 East Center Street, Yreka, CA 96097 • (530) 842-5300. A popular, turn-of-the-century structure, featuring "home-style cooking."

Lewiston Valley Motel, P.O. Box 324, Trinity Dam Blvd., Lewiston, CA 96052 • (530) 778-3942. A pleasant one-story structure with heated swimming pool.

Motel Etna, P.O. Box 754, 317 Collier Way, Etna, CA 96027 • (530) 467-5338. A simple, clean one-story motel.

Mountain Village RV Park, P.O. Box 30, 30 Commercial Way, off Highway 3, Etna, CA 96027 • (530) 467-5678 Paved sites on paved streets in an open grassy field. www.etnarvp.com e-mail: etnarvp@sisqtel.net

Old Lewiston Bridge RV Resort, P.O. Box 148, Lewiston, CA 96052 • (530) 778-3894 •(800) 922-1924 www.lewistonbridgerv.com e-mail: olb@snowcrest.net

Old Lewiston Inn, P.O. Box 688, Lewiston, CA 96052 • (530) 778-3385 • (800) 286-4441. A B&B with 3 rooms in the old Baker House and 4 rooms with decks overlooking the river in a new addition.

Scott River Lodge, P.O. Box 990, 19432 Scott River Road, Fort Jones, CA 96032 • (530) 496-3167. A wilderness retreat, horseman's paradise, rafting and fishing in the Marble Mountains. Expensive but all-inclusive. www.scottriverlodge.com e-mail: scottriverlodge@worldnet.att.net

PART TWO: NORTHEASTERN CALIFORNIA

Bureau of Land Management, California State Office, 2800 Cottage Way, Sacramento, CA 95825 • (916) 978-4400 www.ca.blm.gov

California Department of Fish & Game, 1416 Ninth Street, Sacramento, CA 95814 • (916) 653-7664 www.dfg.ca.gov

Lassen National Forest, 2550 Riverside Drive, Susanville, CA 96130 • (530) 257-2151 www.r5.fs.fed.us/lassen

Modoc National Forest, 800 West 12th Street, Alturas, CA 96101 • (530) 233-5811 www.r5.fs.fed.us/modoc

Plumas National Forest, 159 Lawrence Street, Quincy, CA (530) 283-2050 www.r5.fs.fed.us/plumas

U.S. Fish & Wildlife Service, 4401 N. Fairfax Drive, Arlington, VA 22203 • (800) 344-WILD. For a visitor's guide to wildlife refuges. www.fws.gov

Websites of interest and information:
North State Travel Center   www.shastahome.com
Northern Counties Information Site   www.shastacascade.org

MODOC VOLCANIC SCENIC BYWAY

Dance Country Hall, 104 Pine Street, McCloud, CA 96057 • (530) 964-2578 www.shastahome.com/dance-country

Double Head Ranger District, Modoc NFS, P.O. Box 369, Tulelake, CA 96134 • (530) 667-2246

Heritage Junction Museum, 320 Main Street, McCloud, CA 96057 • (530) 964-2604

Lava Beds National Monument, P.O. Box 867, Tulelake, CA 96134 • (530) 667-2282. Open all year, entrance fee $5 for 7 days, camping fee $10. www.nps.gov/labe

McCloud Chamber of Commerce, P.O. Box 371, 205 Quincy Street, McCloud, CA 96057 •(530) 964-3113   www.mccloudchamber.com

McCloud General Store, 241 Main Street, McCloud, CA 96057 • (530) 964-2934   www.mccloudgeneralstore.com

McCloud Railway Company, P.O. Box 1199, McCloud, CA 96057 • (530) 964-2142 • (800) 733-2121   www.mctrain.com   e-mail: train@mctrain.com

McCloud Golf Course, 1001 Squaw Valley Road, McCloud, CA 96057 • (530)964-2535. Open daily April through November. Pro-shop serves lunch.

Dining and Lodging

Friday's RV Retreat, Squaw Valley Road, P.O. Box 68, McCloud, CA 96057 • (530) 964-2878. e-mail: fridaysrv@snowcrest.net

McCloud Hotel, 408 Main Street, McCloud, CA 96057 • (530) 964-2822 • (800) 964-2823   www.mccloudhotel.com
e-mail: mchotel@snowcrest.net

McCloud Dance-Country RV Park, 480 Highway 89, P.O. Box 486, McCloud, CA 96057   www.mccloudrvpark.com

McCloud River Inn, 325 Lawndale Court, McCloud, CA 96057 • (530) 964-2130 •(800)261-7831   www.mccloudriverinn.com
e-mail: mort@snowcrest.net

McCloud River Lodge, 140 Squaw Valley Road, McCloud, CA 96057 • (530) 964-2700. Lodge dining, The Briar Patch, Mexican Restaurant. www.shastahome.com/mccloud-river-lodge

Raymond's Ristorante, 424 Main Street, McCloud, CA 96057 • (530) 964-2099

SHASTA VOLCANIC SCENIC BYWAY

Burney Chamber of Commerce, 37088 Main Street, Burney, CA 96013 • (530) 335-2111

Butte Valley Chamber of Commerce, 111 Third Street, P.O. Box 531, Dorris, CA 96023 •(530) 397-3771 **www.buttevalleychamber.com** e-mail: contact@buttevalleychamber.com

Fall River Valley Chamber of Commerce, P.O. Box 475, Fall River Mills, CA 96028 •(530) 336-5840 **www.fallriverchamber.net** e-mail: frvchamber@shasta.com

Fort Crook Museum, Fort Crook Avenue, Fall River Mills, CA 96028 • (530) 336-5110

Gooseneck Ranger District, 37805 Highway 97, Macdoel, CA 96058 • (530) 398-4391

Hat Creek Ranger District, Lassen National Forest, P.O. Box 220, Fall River Mills, CA 96028 • (530) 336-5521

Klamath Basin National Wildlife Refuge, 4009 Hill Road, Route 1, Box 74, Tulelake, CA 96143 •(530) 667-2231. Open Monday-Friday 8-4, weekends 10-4. Closed Christmas & New Years. Auto tour, $3 per car; photography blinds, $5 per person. **www.klamathnwr.org**

McArthur-Burney Falls Memorial State Park, Highway 89, 6 miles north of Highway 299, (530) 335-2777

Mt. Shasta Ranger District, 204 W. Alma Street, Mount Shasta, CA 96067 • (530) 926-4511

Mount Shasta Visitors' Bureau and Chamber of Commerce, 300 Pine Street, Mount Shasta, CA 96067 • (530) 926-6212 • (800) 397-1519 **www.mtshasta.com/chamber** e-mail: o-shasta@inreach.com

Oregon Institute of Technology, 1608 Cove Point Road, Klamath Falls, OR 97601 • (800) 445-6728. Yearly conferences on eagles. **www.eagle.org**

Siskiyou Arts Council, 1101 S. Mt. Shasta Blvd. Mount Shasta, CA 96067 • (530) 926-0355 **www.siskiyouarts.com**

Siskiyou County Visitors' Bureau, P.O. Box 1138, Mount Shasta, CA 96067 • (530) 926-3850 **www.visitsiskiyou.org** e-mail: info@visitsiskiyou.org

Sisson Museum, 1 North Old Stage Road, Mount Shasta, CA 96067 • (530) 925-5508

Trails West, Inc. P.O. Box 12045, Reno, NV, 89510 **www.emigranttrailswest.org**

Weed Chamber of Commerce, 34 Main Street, Weed, CA 96094 • (530) 938-4624 **www.weedchamber.com** e-mail: weedchamber@ncen.org

Websites of interest and information:

A huge list of links to birds   www.aviancompanions.com

Birds of Prey Foundation   www.buteo.com

The National Audubon Society   www.birdsource.com

National Scenic Byways   www.byway.org

Northwest Chapter, OR-CA Trails Association   www.nwocta.com

Oregon Institute of Technology annual conference   www.eagle.org

Dining and Lodging

For the Wildlife Refuges; gas, groceries, two motels, and an RV park can be found in Merrill, OR, four miles north of Highway 161 or full services are available in Dorris, CA, Highway 97.

Black Bear Diner, 401 Lake Street, Mount Shasta, CA 96067 • (530) 926-4669   www.blackbeardiner.com
e-mail: blackbeardiner@snowcrest.com

Butte Valley RV Park, 421 E. First Street & Highway 97, P.O. Box 669, Dorris, CA 96023 • (530) 397-7275

Charm Motel, 37363 Main Street, Burney, CA 96013 • (530) 335-2254 www.charmmotel.com e-mail: info@charmmotel.com

Green Gables Motel, 37385 Main Street, Burney, CA 96013 • (530) 335-2264   www.greengablesmotel.com
e-mail: info@greengablesmotel.com

Hi Lo Travelers Complex, 88 S. Weed Blvd., Weed, CA 96094. Motel & RV Park (530) 938-2731; Cafe (530) 938-2904

Lake Siskiyou Camp Resort, 4239 W.A. Barr Road, P.O. Box 276, Mount Shasta, CA 96067 • (530) 926-2618

Pit River Lodge, 24500 Pit One Powerhouse Road, Fall River Mills, CA 96028 • (530) 336-5005. Craftsman style architecturally designed lodge. www.pitriverlodge.com e-mail: stay@pitriverlodge.com

Rancheria RV Park, 15565 Black Angus Lane, Hat Creek, CA 96040 • (530) 355-7418. Open May through October. For reservations, (800) 346-3430. **www.rancheriarv.com** e-mail: ranchrv@c-zone.net

Strawberry Valley Inn, 1142 S. Mount Shasta Blvd., Mount Shasta, Ca 96067 • (530) 926-0842. A single-story B&B on landscaped grounds.

Lodging websites:

Fall River Mills   www.lavacreeklodge.com

Hat Creek fishing resort   www.ripplingwaters.com

Historic hotel in Fall River Mills   www.fallriverhotel.com

LASSEN VOLCANIC SCENIC BYWAY

Almanor Ranger District, P.O. Box 767, Highway 36, Chester, CA, 96020

Chester-Lake Almanor Chamber of Commerce, 529 Main Streets, Chester, CA 96020 • (530) 258-2426 • (800) 350-4838 www.chester-lakealmanor.com   e-mail: almanor@chester-lakealmanor.com

Lassen County Arts Council, 807 Cottage Street, Susanville, CA 96130 • (530) 257-5222. For information about the murals: e-mail: lcarts@thegrid.net

Lassen County Chamber of Commerce, 84 N. Lassen Street, P.O. Box 338, Susanville, CA 96130 •(530) 257-4323   **www.lassencountychamber.org** e-mail: info@lassencountychamber.org

Lassen County Times, 800 Main Street, Susanville, CA 96130 • (530) 257-5321   **www.lassennews.com**   e-mail: lctime@aol.com

Lassen Historical Museum, 75 N. Weatherow Street, Susanville, CA 96130 • (530) 257-3292. Open May-November, Monday-Friday, 10-4.

Lassen Volcanic National Park, P.O. Box 100, Mineral, CA 96063 • (530) 595-4444   **www.nps.gov/lavo**

Susanville Railroad Depot, 601 Richmond Road., Susanville, CA, 96130 • (530) 257-3252. Open Friday-Monday, 9-5.   e-mail: litt@psin.com

Westwood Chamber of Commerce, 463-575 Third Street, Westwood, CA 96137 •(530) 256-2456.   e-mail: waac@thegrid.net

Dining and Lodging

Childs Meadow Resort, 41500 Highway 36E, Mill Creek, CA 96061 • (530) 595-3383. Motel units, chalets, RV sites, store, and cafe. **www.childsmeadowresort.com**   e-mail: visitus@childsmeadowresort.com

Lassen Mineral Lodge, P.O. Box 160, Mineral, CA 96063 • (530) 595-4422. Motel with kitchenettes, restaurant, and general store. **www.minerallodge.com**

St. Bernard Lodge, Highway 36, Mill Creek, CA 96061 • (530) 259-3382. Since 1929, an historic inn, dining and campground. **www.stbernardlodge.com**   e-mail: stbernardlodge@citlink.net

The Bidwell House, #1 Main Street, P.O. Box 1790, Chester, CA 96020 • (530) 258-3338   **www.bidwellhouse.com** e-mail: bidwellhouse.com@thegrid.net

Volcano Country Camping & RV, Highway 36E, Mineral, CA 96063 • (530) 595-3347. **www.volcanocountry.com**